THE COMPETENCE FACTOR

THE COMPETENCE FACTOR

Skills that Make the Difference in Outdoor Sports

Bradford Angier

Stackpole Books

THE COMPETENCE FACTOR

Copyright © 1983 by Bradford Angier

Published by
STACKPOLE BOOKS
Cameron and Kelker Streets
P. O. Box 1831
Harrisburg, PA 17105

Appreciation is expressed for the epigraphs from *Jungle Lore* by Colonel Jim Corbett. Copyright © 1953 by Oxford University Press, Inc.; renewed 1981 by The Standard Bank Ltd. Reprinted by permission of the publisher.

Selected photographs courtesy of:
    The American Red Cross (Mark Stevens)
    Randall Made Knives, Orlando, Florida

Printed in the U.S.A.

Library of Congress Cataloging in Publication Data

Angier, Bradford.
    The competence factor.

    1. Outdoor recreation—Safety measures. I. Title.
GV191.625.A53   1983   796.5028'9   83-4709
ISBN 0-8117-2189-2 (pbk.)

For Remy L. Hudson
—achiever, gentleman, friend—
who has always known what he's doing
and who has always done it best

CONTENTS

III SUMMER

IV AUTUMN

V GETTING IT ALL TOGETHER

Chapter 1

The Outdoor Difference

The outdoors has a quality, apart from the pines and campfire smoke and wolves in the wind-heaving stillness, which makes it different from indoor tracks and bowling alleys. It is that if you are not careful, the outdoors will kill you. Death waits always ready to close in on the unknowing and the unwary.

Each year one of every nine Americans is injured in a participator sport, for the most part avoidably. With 135 million men, women, and young persons already participating in America's outdoor recreation, staying safe in the unpeopled places during every sort of outdoor sport has never been so important.

What others say you can't do outdoors, you may try and find you can. But to stay safe while succeeding, you have to keep ahead of what's happening, anticipating the best but prepared to overcome the worst. Readiness breeds both confidence and caution.

Anyone able to take care of himself or herself is far more likely to turn the difficulties that are part of all outdoor recreation into pleasures. Nothing is more soul-satisfying than the conviction that no matter what may confront you in the unimproved places, you will be able to handle it with skill and sureness to spare.

Even taking to the lakes and woodlands directly from the city can be an advantage. Anybody starting out fresh anywhere, unhampered by acquired false notions and reactions, may have a far better chance of making it away from the masses than many so-burdened country folk. What is often regarded as an inhabitant's natural sense of direction, for example, is ordinarily no more than familiarity with surroundings. This is the major reason explorers historically have been plagued by desertions of aborigine guides. Natives in primitive places have in the main been terrified to venture beyond the areas they have come to know. Yet the greenest beginner who follows some simple direction-determining lore will be able to find his way as surely in one unmarked region as in another.

Many go through life without realizing how much stress and aloneness they can overcome. Discovering your own outer limits is a vital part of being ready. Also, the more knowledge you absorb about self-sufficiency away from the fret of crowded surroundings, the greater becomes your capacity to delight in the exquisite immensities of the forests, mountains, and waters, and the nearer that day comes when you'll savor the ultimate blending of physical ease and mental alertness, possible once solitude can be enjoyed without apprehension.

The skills it takes to get the most satisfaction from recreation are also the ones it takes to make it the safest. Safety outdoors is a positive thing. Endurance is not enough. That is why understanding the basics, which take out the mystery and put in the mastery, can make the difference. Far from being a matter of the survival of the strongest, most often it's the survival of the most knowledgeable.

The most important requirements for staying safe, especially when everything is at stake, are unwavering optimism, certain self-control, unshakable will to live, and knowledge of what to do.

I

WINTER

The book of nature has no beginning, as it has no end. Open the book where you will, and at any period of your life, and if you have the desire to acquire knowledge you will find it of intense interest; and no matter how long or how intently you study the pages your interest will not flag, for in nature there is no finality.

Jim Corbett

Chapter 2

Tactics of Ice Travel

When freezing waterways start to stretch their luring sidewalks through otherwise inaccessible wilderness, the elastic young ice tends at first to bend and crack. Not until it is two inches thick does it become safe for solitary travel. For a group, especially of skaters, it should be twice that thick.

The hardening surfaces of the smaller ponds and lakes usually become passable first. Then the idling brooks firm, in high country sometimes in intriguing series of stairs.

Even during the long winter of night in the Far North, though, the widening sheaths atop the always swiftly flowing rivers remain treacherous after weeks of subzero cold, particularly when water levels keep surging and shrinking. Despite temperatures that drop to more than 60° below 0 Fahrenheit, some frozen stretches remain foggily open and others are skimmed with ice so thin it scarcely supports the shifting whiteness of snow.

AN ELEMENTARY SAFEGUARD

An elementary safeguard when you travel on ice is a long light pole. Carried horizontally in hand or under arm, it can bridge a snow-

Figure 1. A safeguard during ice travel is a long, light pole, carried horizontally so it can automatically bridge a snow-covered hole or a weak spot which lets go, limiting the wetting and providing an escape route.

hidden hole or a weak spot which lets go, limiting the wetting and providing a route of escape. Such poles, frequently located among driftwood or trimmed from a standing dead sapling, also afford the means for prodding safely ahead at suspicious areas perhaps veiled by snow and at frozen shells of overflow covering who knows what.

Staying safe on ice, especially away from the crowded places, is largely a matter of knowing where the dangers are, how to recognize them, and how to take advantage of the resources offered by the countryside.

GETTING OUT AFTER GETTING IN

A threat immediate with breaking through ice poleless where there's current is being swept beneath. If this happens, there's a counteroffensive that, with heartening frequency, provides escape. With your fingers on the remaining rim of ice, immediately begin kicking as if dog-paddling. This serves to bring your body level with the surface. Then, hands and arms spread ahead on what ice is still intact and legs maintaining their impetus, keep striving to squirm and slide flatly forward. Subzero weather can be an advantage in that then wet gloves and sleeves, freezing to the ice on contact, will provide vital purchase.

Initially, more ice may break away, but continuing to press forward with such calculated effort is in most situations, especially when you are on your own, the surest way to reach a place where it will be firm enough to roll beyond the danger area.

THE ADVANTAGES OF PRACTICAL ASSISTANCE

Even when help is at hand, rescuers too often needlessly imperil themselves or let themselves be delayed by weak ice near open water. The most immediate solution is to spread over a wider expanse the weight brought to bear by the lifesaving action. A slower but often

Figure 2. An American National Red Cross Water Safety expert is the "victim" in this demonstration of ice rescue techniques in cooperation with members of the Maryland State Department of Forests and Parks. Foresters have formed a human chain and are using a limb to reach the victim and pull him to safety.

safer stratagem for everyone involved is to keep as much weight as possible away from the accident area.

Occasionally a canoe or flat-bottom boat, cached near the shore for the winter, can be pushed to where whoever's in trouble can grab an end. That close to habitation, even a ladder may be available. More often a sapling or a branch has to serve. When there's a handy vine or line that is awkward to throw, a weighted end generally can be skidded farther and more accurately. Then there's the human chain of rescuers, lying flat and gripping the feet ahead. The lightest or lankiest member stretches to clutch the hapless one and both are hauled safely back.

Getting warm as soon as possible often becomes the primary essential. Such things as sleeping bags, fleecy blankets, and brisk toweling can make this simple. But there still will be that wet clothing. If you are alone in the woods where the best you can do is build a fire, the challenge will be to get it burning before your hands become too numb.

With flames leaping and more fuel within reach, the most comfortable and practical way to dry out may well be with all or most of your clothing on, especially when first you doff it long enough to wring, or if frozen, to beat most of the moisture out.

Often most pleasant in milder weather is to rig a windbreak with the drying garments and enjoy the sybaritic persuasion of heat beating on your bare hide.

Chapter 3

The Steepening Cold

"Freezing to death must be a queer business," said Richard E. Byrd, commanding officer of the United States Antarctic Service. "Sometimes you feel simply great. The numbness gives away to an utter absence of feeling. You are as lost to pain as a man under opium. But at other times, in the unfolding cold, your anguish is the anguish of a man drowning slowly in fiery chemicals."

THE EVERYDAY VIGILANCE OF STAYING UNFROZEN

Few experiences are as exhilarating as the feel of wind, sharp with chill, rustling out of silence enlivened by the thundering concussion of river ice splitting and of trees cracking as the country shrinks from the cold.

You keep feeling your face for any beginning numbness or stiffening. Just as automatically, you stop any starting frostbite by warming the area briefly with a bared warm palm. Then it's a matter of shoving the hand back within its fleecy mitt or, if your fingers are starting to lose their sense of touch, of first clamping the hand in the opposite armpit or pressing it inside your clothing against the skin of your abdomen or chest.

Mitts become such vital weapons in the offense one mounts against the cold that a custom among sourdoughs is to join them with a thong or cord safely looped around the neck.

YOUR FEET CAN MAKE THE DIFFERENCE

You get in the habit of moving your toes. If any ever lose feeling, it's time to stop in the first safe place, get footwear off, dry the feet if necessary, and massage the toes and the rest of the foot. Don't take chances. If it's imperative, build a fire and toast the members comfortably. Then if you've had the forethought to carry them, put on dry socks.

Although damp socks can be hung in the warmth of a little campfire and, with prudence and frequent scrutiny, safely dried, leather is too vulnerable to risk this. It's usually wisest to settle for wiping out the insides of your boots.

Your feet can make the difference when cold is abroad, and usually they are most critically exposed. For a while trench foot accounted for one-third of the Second World War's battlefield casualties admitted to general hospitals in and around Paris. Lieutenant General George Patton sent a memorandum to his commanders in November 1944 which stressed, ''The most serious menace confronting us today is not the German Army, which we have practically destroyed, but the weather which . . . may well destroy us through the incidence of trench foot.''

Even in these days of the insulated rubber boot, trench foot, common to unrelieved contact with wet and cold, remains probably the most widely known of the nonfreezing injuries. Like other injuries, it is seldom, if ever, excusable during recreation outdoors. The world's three highest peaks, after all, have been climbed without cold injury.

VIGILANCE HONED BY COMMON SENSE

Back during the winter of 1777, General George Washington encountered so much difficulty with cold exposure among his men he sent a directive to the officers of the Continental Army urging ''the utmost vigilance.'' Vigilance, honed by common sense, is still what it takes. When you're on your own in remote country, this can mean making camp at the spot.

In the subarctic where I've camped, traveled, and lived for years, buddy systems are seldom practical since the population has long been one human being to every 12½ square miles. Temperatures fall to more than 60° below 0 F., yet no one I know has ever been frozen or even particularly hampered by frigid weather.

THE FACTS OF GETTING UNFROZEN

When severe frostbite, despite its being almost always avoidable, does occur on the trail, it may be well to postpone thawing until the individual is where adequate warmth and comfort can be maintained. Someone otherwise in good condition can at times keep going as long as a day on a frozen foot without further injury. Thawing away from any shelter commonly sets up the very grave risk of refreezing with its far more severe consequences.

Thawing is usually also immediately immobilizing. Often the individual cannot even help in his or her own then far more painful rescue.

TREATMENT ESSENTIALS

A preferred method of treatment, once any urgencies set up by exposure are handled, is rapidly rewarming the involved area for twenty mintues in water kept between 104° F. and 111° F. (40° C. to 44° C.). The International Alpine Rescue Committee recommends initial bathing at about 50° F., with the water's temperature being gradually increased until after half an hour it is 108° F., thereafter maintained. The same temperature range, as well as it can be approximated, is also indicated when thawing by dry heat, such as that from a campfire.

Attempting to rewarm a frozen part by exercise or manipulation is almost sure to increase the extent of the injury. So is any rubbing before, during, or after. This is especially true when, as too often has been done, such rubbing is with snow. Aside from the abrasive effect, the application of one frozen thing to another can hardly help but extend the freezing.

After thawing, further injury to the part should be avoided. Even in extreme cases amputation is rarely advisable in the early stages of the trouble. Not even minor surgery should be attempted in the field on frostbitten tissue.

Recovery depends largely on two things: one is to take care during and after rewarming to avoid further tissue damage; the other is to make a meticulous effort to prevent infection, which after thawing should become the major concern.

THAWING WHERE IT HAPPENS

Outdoors you do the best you can, and this can well be sufficient. Eskimos, although they may feel cold less than most, freeze as quickly as any of us, and igloos in the subzero cold of the Arctic are not noted for having medical facilities nearby.

The first thing to treat is exposure, then the frostbite. While the largest container, if any, of water is being heated, the individual should also be warmed. Anyone so disabled can seldom sustain body heat in extreme cold without external warmth. Even when a nearby tent is reached, it's apt to be pretty bleak. Then not even the finest down sleeping bag, if it hasn't been warmed, will ordinarily be enough. Neither will cold blankets or additional cold clothing.

Best is to get and keep a fire going, day and night, to ensure an evenly comfortable temperature until matters are again right. For the moment, a sleeping bag already warm from somebody else will do. Or get a companion in the bag, too. Hot chocolate, tea, coffee, or broth will help. Whatever, keeping the victim warm and assured will brighten the situation considerably.

WARM WATER OR WRAPPING

Where thawing with warm water is practical, the optimum temperature is 112°F. (44°C.), checked, when not by a thermometer, by unimpaired fingers or preferably an elbow, never by the injured area. As soon as the water is ready, the bared frozen part should be immersed. The optimum soaking time is twenty minutes.

The larger the volume of liquid, the longer it will withstand chilling. More water heated in a second receptacle, never over 115°F., can be safely added as often as rechecking indicates is necessary to maintain the desired temperature. The one precaution is not to pour the water too near the injured member. Keeping the container over the fire instead of adding water to keep it warm is far more tricky and hazardous.

When no container is available in which the frozen part can be wholly submerged, wrap this area with towels over which warm water within the same temperature range, never hotter than 112°F, or 44°C., is steadily poured.

Generally, any such rapid rewarming is not particularly uncomfortable during the first ten minutes, especially when one is young and hardy. During the remaining ten minutes pain gradually builds, although not unbearably. Circulatory disability and age, however, can increase its severity.

Two five-grain aspirin tablets, repeated if needed at four-hour intervals, will safely reduce the distress in most instances without any interference with healing.

CAMPFIRE CARE

Where liquid treatment is not possible, similarly moderate warmth from a fire can be the solution. Intense heat from any source should be very carefully avoided. Even excessive use of dry campfire heat is almost sure to cause additional damage, sometimes gangrene.

Where there's not even a little fire, an overcold foot may be warmed against your own bared thigh. Or, better, a companion may offer a warm abdomen. On the tundra the occasional prospector and trapper, as a last resort, kills and opens the steaming inside of a caribou and sometimes even a sled dog.

Any such thawing is best completed in one effort. This is apt to be three or four times longer than the water method. In any event, you do the best you can, which usually turns out to be enough.

FOLLOWING THE THAWING

Afterwards, cleaning the area can help, with water where there's the opportunity. Boil this water first when there's any question of purity, at least five minutes at sea level and one more minute for each additional thousand feet of altitude. Mild soap and gentle dabbing, with a soft cloth that is also sterile, work well together.

Then keeping the part uncovered is best wherever the air is both temperate and clean. The thawed area should be allowed to remain at its own natural body temperature.

The softest and lightest available dry dressings are desirable if the thawed part is to be covered. Experience has shown the inadvisability of cutting off any tissue at this stage.

When kept undisturbed and clean even the skin which seems most seriously injured often heals against all apparent odds. The advice is never to open even a blister. What's proved to be best, especially in remote regions, has been leaving the area entirely alone except for replacing any dressings, and not changing these unless they become too disturbingly unkempt.

Frequent, voluntary, and very cautious gentle movement of all involved joints will help keep muscles, ligaments, and tendons flexible until, often without any loss of tissue whatsoever, the most miserable looking foot will slough its withered blackness as painlessly as a sock, abruptly uncovering sound, fresh skin beneath.

Maintaining a successful offensive against cold is mostly a matter of alertness and common sense. If you have ever been frostbitten, take into account your now being more susceptible, particularly in the previously affected part.

Whenever you can, keep the extent of any injury limited by keeping your tetanus boosters current.

TALL-COUNTRY PROBLEMS

Keeping clear of cold injury depends, everywhere, on the heat-manufacturing capacity your body maintains and on the effectiveness with which you conserve this heat once it's produced.

In the higher altitudes the inborn protective mechanism of shivering, among other things, is often impaired to such an extent that even this self-warming process may not be present to help.

Also, precisely the same amount of oxygen is needed by the human system to handle a given task at any altitude. Yet the higher you climb, the more air your lungs with their three hundred million to four hundred million air cells must process to extract this vital element. Larger and larger amounts of body warmth are lost just during the panting brought on by increased exertion.

If anyone inadequately clothed and nourished is stopped by exhaustion or injury in severe cold, it can become impossible in the higher altitudes for the body to maintain a level of self-warming sufficient for the situation.

Once one's heat output diminishes below the subsistence level, the body slows the blood flow to the skin and extremities in a last-chance attempt to retain normal temperature at its core. The stage approaches when no quantity of insulation can prevent even frostbite. Then only rigorous warming from an external heat source, along with oxygen if that is available, can forestall increasingly serious consequences. The use of oxygen above twenty-four thousand feet, even on climbs preceded by acclimatization, has a proved linkage with freezing prevention.

Chapter 4

Cold-Country Adventuring

When an old hand begins feeling more like a relic than a legend when skiing, snowshoeing, or slogging into the chill dazzle of sunset, it's time for caution, particularly as it is only human to disregard the reality that susceptibility to hypothermia increases with age.

When any of us, for that matter, is occupied by the challenge of covering ground, exhaustion sometimes creeps in unrecognized. This can be so much more serious a problem in severe weather that just staying safe can depend upon making camp early enough to prepare sufficiently protective cover and, if possible, to eat.

Short of a solo miscalculation as extreme as breaking through the snow-veiled ice of a timberline lake, and by no means necessarily then, hypothermia among the free and healthy is rarely justified. Blizzard? Lost? The answer outdoors everywhere is still to hope confidently for the best, but always to be prepared for overcoming the worst. A bonus is the atavistic satisfaction there is in being ready.

When companions are along, a reassuring backup can be everyone watching everyone else. The idea is to make it appear all-important that each member of a party accepts the responsibility for recognizing any early signs and symptoms of hypothermia in the others. However, another obligation is a lot more basic. Self-reliance will get you further than depending on someone else, unless you plan to go through life in a crowd.

HYPOTHERMIA

Hypothermia is encountered in low temperatures. When one is unwary, unwitting, unfortunate, or unprepared, it can be made increasingly immediate by wind, weather, and trying to tough it out with too little water and food. Too often, the individual doesn't realize how vital it is to maintain adequate body fluid content or even that eating snow can also help, and he or she keeps going without drinking sufficient water. The result can be subnormal temperature within the midbody, below the level which the vital organs there need to continue functioning normally.

Hypothermia by whatever name can overtake anyone not consciously or even subconsciously ready for it, and can happen anywhere, from vacation country such as the sweeping lowland forests to the steepening mountains, as well as in their icy waters.

There is far less excuse, though, when you're afoot and dry among the tall peaks or the sheltering woodlands below. Although numerous people do go overboard unexpectedly, there is seldom any surprise to being in cold back country, short of crash-landing there in a plane.

WARNINGS

Indications of developing trouble may be undue fatigue, weakness, apathy, forgetfulness, sluggishness, confusion, and slowing gait. Shivering is not always evident, especially in rigorous going. Muscular incoordination and mental impairment settle in when hypothermia becomes serious. In its later stages the individual is cold, pale, stiff, and breathing more and more shallowly and slowly.

Handling such difficulty early ordinarily reverses the pattern in anyone fit enough to be actively enjoying such outdoor recreation in the first place. Anyone accustomed to cold-country adventuring on his or her own ordinarily is soon aware of any onset of hypothermia and, without putting a name to it, handles the situation as a matter of course before the trouble has a chance to progress dangerously.

THE PERILOUS PATTERN

Muscular and cerebral dysfunction are a result of what starts out as surface cold extending into the vital-organ structure of the inner body.

All warm-blooded mammals have built-in thermostats. Among human beings, these keep our body temperature generally within half a degree of 98.6 F. Our nervous systems react to outside thermal fluxuations by changing the flow of blood to the skin. Thus we respond to heat by perspiring and are cooled through evaporation. To cold we often respond by shivering and are warmed through the muscular activity.

This involuntary self-regulation of body temperature lets those of us who opt for it thrive happily in the Arctic and Antarctic, as well as along the sweltering equator. It operates within certain limits. Below or above this range, any of us will be in trouble.

Muscles lose their ability to coordinate when the body cools some five degrees. At lower temperatures, mental difficulty appears. Between 82°F. and 78°F., effective heart function falters.

Such core temperatures cannot be determined by the usual thermometer, which is neither charged nor even calibrated to register such cold. Hypothermia thermometers, as well as thermometers to measure hyperthermia from heat, are now being imported from England by Dr. William W. Forgey. The former reads as low as 70°F., the latter as high as 115°F. Both are available from Indiana Camp Supply, Inc., Pittsboro, Indiana, 46167.

Ordinarily, the presence and the extent of hypothermia can be detected solely by the visible signs of progressive muscular, intellectual, and circulatory disorder.

An early warning may be apparently unwarranted fatigue, one of the danger signals for which to be alert whenever predisposing environmental and personal factors exist. Other symptoms include weakness, blundering, apathy, sluggishness, forgetfulness, confusion, incoherence, and difficulty even with just keeping pace.

When one's movements lose coordination and mental deterioration becomes apparent, the insidious internal chilling may already be critical. Abnormally lowering blood pressure can leave the individual unnaturally pale. Stiffness may become pronounced, along with a fixity of widened pupils and shortening breath still slowing more.

The time span in some instances is unnervingly short. The interval between the first recognizable inroads and collapse can be as brief as one hour. Such abrupt helplessness may be followed within another two hours by death.

STAY-SAFE SOLUTIONS

Early recognition, a prompt counteroffensve, and in advanced cases the maintenance of rewarming for as long as it takes for the midbody temperature to become normal (possibly several hours) can make the difference.

Unless a cabin, tent, or other shelter is close, a bivouac should be made at the nearest safe spot and treatment started. The axiom? Where you are, with what you have, right now! A slit scooped in windswept snow, especially with a fire at one end, can do.

The problem in even the more favorable surroundings quickly becomes reversing the drop in central temperature without bringing about shock. Rough handling may be enough to start the overchilled surface blood, now also impaired with metabolic waste, flowing back into the midbody with endangering speed. A consequence can be disrupted heart performance, with pulse and heartbeats disasterously losing their synchronization.

A desirable procedure is to gently move and disrobe an otherwise healthy individual and to allow him to rewarm under a soft cover in comfortably heated quarters, closely attended during the critical first half hour when mouth-to-mouth respiration may be needed.

Outdoors, a sleeping bag from a backpack can serve if the individual is undressed with all practical solicitude and made dryly snug within. Because even the finest prime northern white goose down only insulates and does not warm, a heat source other than the cold victim's presently inadequate body needs to be provided. Stones or sufficiently full canteens, warmed in the campfire and then safely wrapped or shoved inside heavy socks to prevent burning, can help. Direct contact with a warm companion is better. Boughs stripped from a nearby spruce or other conifer will serve as insulation between sleeping bag and frozen ground. Also, try to protect any exposed areas of the individual, such as head and neck, from the frosty air.

When the individual is sufficiently conscious to swallow, steaming drinks like tea and hot chocolate can significantly speed recovery. Keep away from anything alcoholic, even when it's first heated. After perhaps some momentary sensation of warmth, alcohol promotes overall heat loss through the skin by dilating the blood vessels.

Throughout, commonsense actions should be geared to conditions. Although at the start clothes might be less roughly and more swiftly cut free than removed intact, this would not be desirable in back country where the recovered individual would need them on the way out. Also, unless something like a blanket or a down bag is at hand, wet woolens, in wind especially, are markedly warmer than bare hide. They're even warmer if a good part of the water is pressed or wrung out. This is true despite the generally accepted belief that heat loss may be increased by a factor of more than thirty when the skin is wet or exposed to wet clothing.

Chapter 5

Morning, Winter, and Night

Making a winter camp in open country on the side of an elevation which is out of the wind, a natural enough precaution in the woods, can in these emptier regions get you in trouble. These lees in terrain such as the tundra and plains tend to gather overnight drifts often deep enough to bury a tent and suffocate whoever's sleeping within.

SNOWSLIDE ESCAPE

Eroded ravines and open slopes unstable with fresh or melting snow are areas to travel gingerly, if at all, during winter and the nearing spring. Experience increases ability to assess their ever changing avalanche hazard. In the meantime, your safety is best assured by such detours as the often handy ridges.

If you are overtaken by a snowslide, you will still have a good chance to turn the encounter into no more than adventure, particularly if you can keep on top of the smashing, bulging, swirling, and bellying surge. One way to accomplish this is with swimming movement. The backstroke, especially effective when it can be done, has saved lives in such crises.

Just drawing your head, arms, and legs together in the huddle or fetal position can provide an air pocket. Then, if you're close enough to the surface for daylight to filter through when the sliding stops, but not close enough for it to indicate the way out, wad a fistful of snow and watch which way it falls. If it is too dark for that, saliva or urine may still indicate the direction up into the glorious open air.

ROCK FALL AND AVALANCHE

A greater danger in gullies and ravines is sudden rock fall. The threat freshens during seasonal thaw and more briefly while, and immediately after, there's heavy rain. Some of the sheerer faces spew stone intermittently, others seldom do so except during the drying and expanding impetus of sunlight. Debris along the floors of the narrow valleys and overhung canyons, or fanned out at a gorge's base, are warnings. If you see these signs, keep to the middle or seek at least a broader couloir.

Even when such a sign is covered with snow, the pitting effects of its still relatively greater absorption of heat are often evident on the surface. Long downward ruts in slanting steepnesses above always merit suspicion.

THE ADVANTAGE OF EATING SNOW

The loss of integral body moisture through the lungs is intensified in cold weather as a result of breathing more dry air. For this reason you need to ingest more water. Another reason to drink more water is the negative perspiration factor, which causes the kidneys to take over much of the function of eliminating body wastes accomplished in warmer temperatures by the sweat glands.

The approximately two quarts of water you need daily can be as near as the handfuls of snow easy to scoop up while going along. Clean ice and snow normally can be safely consumed as long as you don't take in too much too quickly when overchilled or overheated.

Otherwise, unless one is carrying a canteen or occasionally stopping to build a fire, the tendency is to keep pressing on and wondering why he or she feels more and more overtired.

CLOTHING SECURITY

Burdening yourself in heavy clothes may be relatively harmless on frosty mornings in the city. In the wilderness it can kill you. Excessive perspiring, as from dressing too warmly during subzero weather in proportion to exertion, is something to avoid in unfrequented regions.

If your garb does not permit adequate escape of perspiration always present to some extent, it can freeze inside the clothing in very cold weather. Besides being unpleasant, this can reduce the insulating efficiency of your garb to an unsafe, if not endangering, extent.

A practical solution is the layer system. Leave camp warmly dressed and then shed layers as things heat up, stowing this apparel in a light backpack for gradual redonning once temperatures reverse. Another stratagem which betters with experience is opening garments before you begin to sweat and closing them before you really feel chilly.

The quality down-filled and windproof clothes afford the most flexibility in extreme weather. It's the combination of wind with cold that is the major danger. The chilling effect of a 20°F. morning, suddenly filled with a forty-five-mile-an-hour gale, becomes identical with 40° below 0 F. weather in a two-mile-an-hour breeze.

THE SUNBURNS OF WINTER

The higher the country, the more ultraviolet light the atmosphere leaves unfiltered. When there are snowfields and glaciers, these reflect about three-fourths of the already burdensome unfiltered light, increasing solar irradiation further. The thin cirrus clouds often present add to the scattering of the total onslaught at ground levels.

Today's recreationists are capitalizing more and more on creams and lotions containing screening agents, such as the para-aminobenzoic preparations. These help to prevent sunburn at high altitudes by absorbing the ultraviolet light within the 290–320 nanameter spectrum. Excessive exposure to this causes the trouble. The products usually also enhance new pigment formation. Individuals particularly susceptible also use such blocking ingredients as titanium dioxide and zinc oxide on the nose and other higher risk areas.

Treatment, when still necessary, includes the cold saline compresses available almost everywhere, emollients to soothe and relieve dryness, and locally applied topical corticosteroid lotions, creams, gels, and sprays to reduce inflammation and pain.

Chapter 6

Safeguarding Your Visual System

Your visual system controls your motive system. That is, the way you move depends on what you see.

One-fifth of the eyes' function in skiing, for example, goes toward maintaining balance. Reaction time to this and every fast-moving situation on the slopes and everywhere else is slowed, often dangerously, when sight is impaired even briefly by such deterrents as glare and fogged glasses.

THE CASE FOR CONTACTS

A solution to fogging problems, especially when corrective glasses have to be worn, is contact lenses for those who can use them. Now that the soft plastics have come along, so have more and more contact wearers. Over ten million Americans, it's been estimated, now wear contact lenses. Sales of the flexible plastic contacts have been growing by about 25 percent a year.

The advantages of the flexible varieties for athletic participation are more initial comfort, greater resistance to displacement, less tendency to cause abrasion when there's direct injury, and a lower risk of foreign bodies becoming lodged beneath.

There are also the increasingly effective liquids for keeping regular glasses clear. One such product, Fogmaster, reaches into outer space. It is based on a formula first used during the Apollo moon shot.

SAFETY IN SNOW-COUNTRY GLASSES

Distortion-free lenses of impact-resistant glass or scratch-proof plastic with warranted ultraviolet protection are the safest glasses for recreational wear in snow country everywhere.

They are also the best there is for sports such as skiing. This is particularly evident in the steeper and swifter places when skiers' fields of view are large and uninterrupted. Soft flexible nosepads, particularly those with adjustable widths, can help too by minimizing slippage when air pressure is high.

Plastic frames do not become as cold against the face as metal ones. Plastic frames should be sturdy, agreeably lightweight, firm fitting, and made to lessen distracting light reflection. Darkening about, and especially under, the eyes, perhaps on the spot with charcoal from a campfire, can further reduce light reflection.

Sunglasses which clip over prescription lenses may damage them. Besides, except directly in front, they do not adequately cut snow and ice glare.

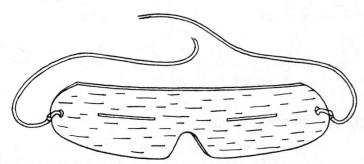

Figure 3. Primitive "sunglasses" you can fashion from bark, fabric, or bone provide safe glare protection and don't fog or frost over.

TARGETS AND SAFE EYES

Shatterproof shooting glasses, especially those with zero-power lenses which neither magnify nor reduce, are safest overall. The higher bridges on the better models raise the lenses higher on the forehead, so that looking through rather than over them when sighting down a gun barrel is more natural.

Even inexpensive plastic safety glasses, as well as sunglasses and the shooters' own prescription lenses, afford protection.

Yet not trusting less than the best shooting glasses available makes more sense in situations where fragments of case and primer metal, burning powder grains, excess lubricants, and even ejected cases could strike the naked eyes.

Today's shooting glasses are available in a spectrum of lens colors, which can make targets stand out more distinctly against certain backgrounds and in different conditions of light and brightness.

Vermillion, for example, in addition to reducing harmful ultraviolet radiation, provides orange-red visual adaption, helpful when hitting the orange trap targets frequently used on overcast days and during the intriguing low-level hours near dawn and dusk.

WHICH HUE WILL DO

Because vision is so important to coordination, reflexes, and concentration, participants in the faster moving recreations particularly are seeking the most functional colors in eyewear. An example is what's more available for the swiftly varying conditions in ice and snow regions.

Gray, essentially a neutral filter, is highly regarded for its integrity in color perception. Dark gray lenses are a frequent choice for winter's brisk sunny days. A concern other times is that they not be overly dark, for too little light likewise can cause problems, such as making terrain unduly difficult to read. Green, which eliminates harmful ultraviolet rays and blocks infrared's heat radiation, is nearly as efficient. Yellow is helpful when there's ground fog and during overcast days when you can cope, too, in the faster moving sports by slowing your action and by keeping your gaze moving.

WIDENING PERIPHERAL VISION

Good peripheral vision becomes even more of a safeguard when there's dwindling visibility.

To improve visibility during off-hours, hold a ruler, with a white patch of paper stuck to one end, at eye level with the arm fully extended. Close one eye, then follow the paper with the other while moving the patch sideways as far as it can be seen in either direction. Repeat with the other eye. Ideally, the exercise should be done about five minutes daily.

SEEING DURING SNOWBLINDNESS

Sunlight, its ultraviolet and infrared rays already more intense in the drier and thinner air of the higher altitudes, not only transiently obscures insufficiently protected vision with glare, but also can set up seriously disabling long-range complications.

One such complication is snowblindness, which is not blindness at all, its victims discover, but a watery and painful inflammation. The condition is one result of overexposure to certain ultraviolet radiants which are so diffused by water particles, frozen or not, that brightness assails the eyes from every direction. The same syndrome is set up in warm temperatures, on the beaches and away from water entirely in arid desert intensity.

You are not ordinarily aware of anything but brilliance. When the symptoms do appear, as long as twelve hours later, your eyes begin feeling dry, irritated, and at times so sandy that pain accompanies eyeball movement and even blinking. Inflammation of the mucous membrane lining the inner surface of the lids spreads over the foreparts of the eyes, and there's swelling and increased tearing.

Treatment includes cold compresses and avoiding sunlight until matters right themselves. When the occurrence is severe, bandaging can help. Keeping your eyes closed doesn't always give enough protection for optimum results, not even inside the usual tent. Bathing the eyes with cold weak tea has been found soothing by sourdoughs in the Alaskan and Canadian North, where frequently they follow this up with cold packs made with the tea leaves remaining.

Skiers, as a whole better equipped than others, have discovered that frequent application of ophthalmic ointment containing corticosteroids usually decreases inflammation and shortens the course of the photophthalmia or snowblindness.

Local anesthetics should not be used, cautions skiing and practicing Seattle physician Eric B. Larson. Even without medication, including tea's dilute tannic acid, the condition ordinarily resolves with time.

Best is avoidance, handily accomplished by sunglasses transmitting less than 10 percent of the ultraviolet rays under 320 nanometers.

Goggles, or at least glasses with side guards, insure the fullest practical protection readily available. Next are the sometimes individually preferred oversize lenses when these are well fitted and not too far from the face.

SEEING AND SAFETY

Unimpaired vision while snowmobiling becomes increasingly critical in ratio with acceleration, as in the deadly instance of barbed wire. With disturbing frequency such strands are being discovered too late, strung around bare fields and meadows, along unsuspected property lines, and around wooded lifestock enclosures in regions so remote they look like just more wilderness.

Glasses, contact lenses, goggles, and face shields, with the same safety characteristics examined elsewhere in conjunction with skiing, cycling, and shooting, are important also for safe snowmobiling. So, in many situations, are the helmets of skiing and cycling.

Chapter 7

That One More Slope

The flexibility so necessary in skiing for responding quickly to surface and terrain changes, and in some instances absorbing them, decreases with mounting fatigue. Tiring and increasingly careless, you lose more and more reflex and conscious resilience, vital for adjusting to stress and shock without damage to muscle and bone.

Most dangerous is the first day on the slopes. Next is that impulsive one more run.

SKIING AND STAYING SAFE

The possum's determination to stay alive is believed unequalled by any other mammal, including humans. The cerebral processes of this continent's oldest wild animal do run into trouble, however, when it comes to separating its body's reflexes. Mental muscle like that of our sole marsupial wouldn't get anyone far with the safety-related skills of skiing. Fortunately there are other approaches to skiing safely. In any event, the sport is booming.

The nearly 29 percent gain in one year recently showing up in purchases by cross-country advocates has been accompanied by a sim-

35

ilar rise in Nordic equipment sales, which lifts the total into the billion dollar range. With buying of Alpine or downhill gear reported by re-tailers to be holding even, indications are that the more leisurely phase of skiing may soon overtake downhill's popularity.

The cross-country enthusiasts, 6.7 million by recent count against the downhillers' 11 million, do not need mountains and so avoid the long drives, the lifts, and the greater risks of disability expenses.

Women's soaring involvement in outdoor recreation is having more and more impact on national sales of skiing gear. A study by New York advertising agency Benton & Bowles showed nearly 45 percent of all downhill skiers (and for that matter 49 percent of all tennis players and 36 percent of those who enjoy squash) are now women. One hearty boon to staying safe is that the trend in feminine taste has shifted from fashionable to functional sportswear.

THE PRECONDITIONING SOLUTION

Skiing and staying sound can depend to a large degree on precon-ditioning aimed directly toward the demands of this sport.

The first thing to determine, suggested Dr. John L. Marshall, late head of the Sports Medicine Service at New York's Hospital for Special Surgery, is whether you are loose-jointed or tight-jointed. Feminine skiers, he noted, more often are loose-jointed than are men.

Loosely coupled skiers need strong muscles around the joints, particularly in the shoulders, ankles, and hips. The tight-jointed, who are more prone to muscle pulls, require greater muscle flexibility to ski safely at top capacity.

Those tending to be loose find they can perform these flexibility tests easier: 1) Touch your forearm with that hand's thumb. 2) With knees straight, bend your feet upward at a 20° to 30° angle. 3) Sit with your legs crossed and each foot atop the opposite thigh in the familiar lotus position.

FOR STRONGER LEG MUSCLES

To strengthen the calf muscles, so important to cross-country skiing, stand for several seconds on the ball of one foot with the other foot slightly raised. Then lower the foot and stand one-legged on it. Repeat with the other leg. Add to this sequence daily. (See Fig. 4A.)

A way toward stronger muscles in the backs of the thighs is to stand on one leg with a weight attached to the ankle of the other.

A.

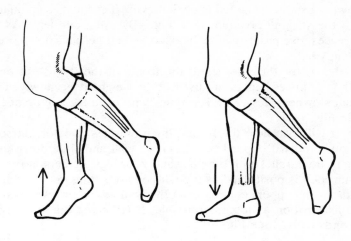

B

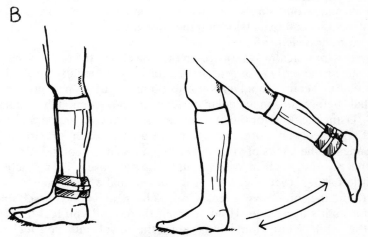

Figure 4A. To strengthen calf muscles, stand on the ball of one foot with the other raised behind you. Then slowly lower your foot and stand flat-footed with the other still raised. Repeat several times, changing feet.

Figure 4B. For stronger muscles in the backs of the thighs, stand with one leg free and with a weight attached to the other. Slowly raise the weighted leg behind you. Then just as gradually, lower it. Alternate legs, using a progressively heavier weight.

Slowly raise the weighted leg behind you. Then just as gradually lower it to the starting position. (See Fig. 4B.) Alternate legs. As strength increases, use progressively heavier weight, perhaps just more sand in a handy ski sock.

Next, for the muscles in the fronts of the thighs, sit on a chair with your knees bent naturally. Lift the weighted leg slowly. Then with equal slowness, lower it. Ten times with each leg will do at the start. (See Fig. 5A.)

It will also help the frontal thigh muscles, Doctor Marshall said, if you stand with your back against a wall and slide down until your thighs are parallel with the floor and your legs are bent at right angles. Your body is positioned as though you are sitting in a straight-backed chair, with support coming from the wall and your own legs. Remain in this position as long as possible, lengthening this time five to ten seconds daily. (See Fig. 5B.)

HAMSTRING STRETCHES FOR STRETCHING YOUR SAFETY

Dangers increase progressively during downhill runs in ratio with tiring thigh muscles, particularly those not in condition even at the start. These hamstrings and quadriceps, the source of upper thigh pain among numerous skiers, are what you must control during repeated contractions and expansions on the way down if even the easier slopes are to be traveled safely.

Two practical ways to stretch the muscles at the back of the thighs are suggested by Doctor Marshall, a former orthopedist for the United States Ski Team. He advises not to bounce during their progress and to halt before these particular muscles are pulled enough to hurt.

Using the floor for the first routine, sit with your legs straight ahead and your heels no more than six inches apart. Reach forward until the muscles in the backs of your thighs begin feeling uncomfortable. Relax in this position, as best you can, until the pull eases. Then reach ahead a little farther. (See Fig. 6A.) A towel can make this easier. Just loop it around the soles of your feet. Grip each end and pull yourself forward as far as it's agreeable. Hold yourself there until you feel ready for a further pull. Work your hands down the towel until you feel you're sufficiently stretched for each repeated session.

The second method involves a wall, table, tree, or such. With the leg straight, place a heel against the upright as high as you can comfortably reach. The leg on which you're standing should be at least nearly straight, with its foot pointed forward. (See Fig. 6B.) Any back problems may be eased by bending this knee, a concession best kept

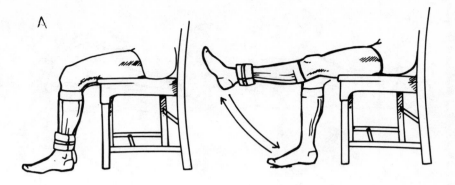

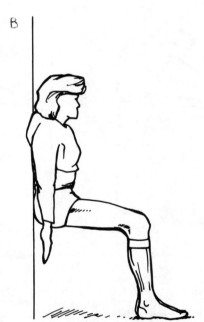

Figure 5A. For stronger frontal thigh muscles, put a weight on one ankle and sit on a chair with your knees bent naturally. Slowly lift the weighted leg. Then slowly lower it. Ten times with each leg will do at the start.

Figure 5B. It will also help strengthen these frontal thigh muscles if you sit on the floor with your back flat against a wall and legs bent at right angles as though you were sitting in a straight-backed chair. Remain in this position as long as you can, lengthening this time five to ten seconds daily.

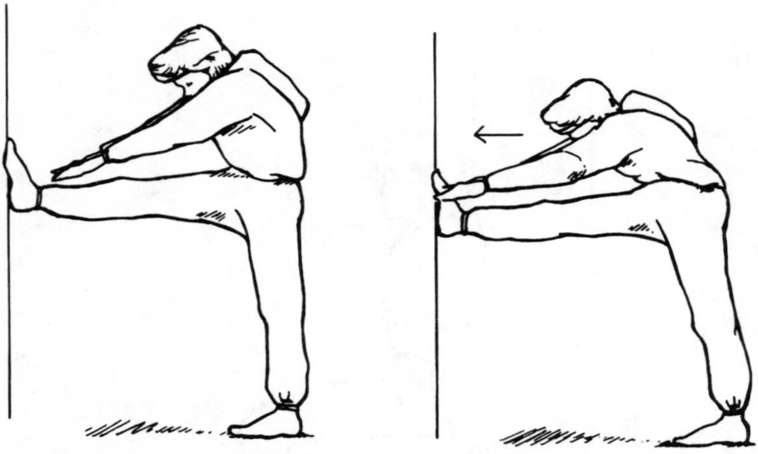

Figure 6A. To stretch the back thigh muscles, sit on the floor with legs straight ahead and heels no more than six inches apart. Reach forward until these muscles start feeling uncomfortable. Relax, then reach ahead a bit more.

Figure 6B. Another hamstring stretcher involves standing and lifting one leg as high as you comfortably can while keeping it straight, the heel against a wall. Keeping the leg on which you're standing nearly straight, bend slowly forward from the waist, relaxing during the initial stretches until any undue discomfort eases. Press a little farther forward, then switch legs.

as minimal as possible. Then bend slowly forward from the waist, relaxing as during the initial stretches until any undue pull eases. Afterward, press a little closer to the elevated leg. Then do the same thing while standing on the other foot. Continuing and lengthening this routine day after day should give you more and more of an advantage.

THE SAFETY SKID

On downward slopes too perpendicular to invite even zigzagging, controlling the momentum of a sideslip with the entire bite of your edges can keep it within safe limits. This can be especially practical when you moderate the lateral slide by increasing the angle at which the bottoms press into the slant, while keeping your weight well over the skis.

Even if you lean too far into the hill and fall, matters needn't go badly. You can usually get your skis out of the way, aloft and behind, and your arms widespread to help slow you down. You can slow yourself down more quickly when your clothes have the added deceleration factor that's built into much of the present ski garb. At worst, the glancing slide rather than the impact of stopping short, the cushioning snow, and today's safety bindings usually make the rest mostly a matter of staying loose.

THE SWASHBUCKLING TRAVERSE

The traverse can be a more swashbuckling and less defensive way of getting out, as well as keeping out, of such downhill difficulty.

Tactics for this maneuver include maintaining a wider distance between your skis for added stability and lessened entanglement risk, at the same time keeping your arms out sideways for surer balance. Then it's a matter of steadying about two-thirds of your weight on the downhill ski, rather than heeding any instinct to lean toward the slope with probably more than a third of your weight on the upper one. This is not so much because you might fall, but because of the greater possibility of uncontrolled tumbling if you do.

STOPPING IN TIME

The rest of the time the way out may be a turn toward the slope in the likelier direction if you want to slow or stop.

When a stop must be sudden, instead of pressing ahead with knees and hips to finish the swerve, an alternate can be keeping your shoulders at right angles to the slant and your skis skidding almost straight downward on their sides. Once you have all this together, cut your rims into the slope as sharply as they will bite and, knees braced forward, rasp to a halt.

To begin the maneuver, lean into the slope, body nearly erect and lower hand high, and concentrate muscle and balance in absorbing the

Figure 7. A safe, sudden downhill stop can be made by keeping the shoulders at right angles to the slant of your skis, skidding almost directly downward on their sides. Cut your rims into the slope as sharply as they will bite and, knees braced forward, rasp to a halt.

decreasing momentum. If this isn't too great, a standstill will be almost instantaneous. With more speed, there will be some sideslipping first.

The technique is most safely mastered on the gentler inclines, when you don't need it. Then when you do, it may avert mayhem.

CRASH HELMET

Speed isn't the danger. Skiing out of control is, especially when you cannot stop or even change direction within your range of visibility.

Downhill, when two waxed strips are all there is between you and a heaving, jolting iciness screeching underneath sometimes more than seventy-five miles per hour, a crash helmet can help.

THE POWDER GAME

The hazards of venturing first through fresh powder snow may seem surprisingly small in relation to the exhileration, which among some skiers is surpassed only by jumping. But the preventive offenses to take are relatively minor, too.

Powder snow, unlike harder surfaces where there's usually time to redirect a ski straying out of line, tends to entrap an erring edge quickly and then, swiftly and inescapably, bury the rest. What can help, along with more attention to the path you're cutting, is the awareness that when turning, your weight is more prudently carried equally on each ski. This is unlike the practice on more solid footing of putting the greater heft on the one outside.

There's also the matter of compensating for powder's instability by unweighing with a directed rather than a more natural up-and-down motion, controlled not at the waist but at the bending and unbending knees. Leaning toward the fall line from the waist, while pointing the poles the same way with increased arm action, can make all this help. Letting them get behind too often sets up a soon catching edge.

A positive approach to the possibility of rocks and downfall being concealed in unexplored powder is allowing your weight to tend more toward your heels. Your ski tips then can plane better. Any inclination to press forward instead, especially with your upper body, can so overbalance the odds that your tips will dig in with an almost inevitable result.

SKIRTING THE CROWDED SLANTS

Something to keep in mind when keeping away from the crowds and their ruts by skiing the borders is that rim snow remains less disturbed in part because of the increased possibility of snags hidden beneath. Also there's generally more threat of swerving into trees.

The response to such hazards is skiing under control, and capitalizing on the usual travel-built bank by using it to begin your turns. Then even as you may be nearing trouble, you'll be starting your return to a safer area.

When the mountain seems everywhere tracked, tree-surrounded open places still often remain unmarked despite their being within bounds. Here shadows perhaps have preserved the powder of a former week's snowfall. While staying excitingly alert, make round turns around the visible obstacles that at any moment you can change to stops, glide always far enough from any possibly entrapping dents left by the shade, and lean well enough back to keep your points planing in the relatively formless and challengingly unfathomable cover.

Or there may be gullies, to swoop down on one side and with slowing momentum up the other, wary that some other loner, reveling in the same enjoyment of gravitation, does not bank into you headlong.

Momentums, planes, separations, and constantly reversing fall lines can be deceptive in much gully skiing. But a bank, to sweep up to a carefree halt is almost always close.

SPACE BENEATH YOUR FEET

Crowning overhangs, molded by winds blowing snow across precipitous drops, become deathtraps each winter on the sheltered crests. This snow the swooping gales sweep from a gentler incline.

Ridges with one gradual side and the other steep are most conducive to the formation of cornices. Along the crowns of such ranges, their inviting flatness can be particularly beguiling to a skier who has reached the top from the moderate slope and never suspects part of such a table is suspended over emptiness. Caution born of the awareness that there are cornices, with the resulting attention to ridge formation in the area and to such immediate warnings as surface cracks, can keep the skier from venturing beyond the breakage line.

Cornices can become especially hazardous when the skier's attention is otherwise occupied, as when selecting some untried ridge as a prudent alternate route around avalanche hazard.

Following all unfamiliar snow-clad ridges well toward their windward sides is the surest safeguard.

Chapter 8

To Snowmobile Next Winter, Too

Now that snowmobiling has become the third fastest growing sport in America, with more participants already than either cross-country or downhill skiing, there is a widening bi-national concern. It is the growing problem of staying safe on and off the some quarter of a million miles of public and private snowmobile trails which extend across the top of this country and throughout much of Canada.

The significance of this hazard can be gauged in part by the way the trail system is expanding. This is showing up in such wide expanses as Quebec's, whose thirty-five thousand miles of snowmobile routes exceed the total length of the province's highways, and in the more localized areas, such as in and around Yellowstone National Park where maintained snowmobile ways reach over one thousand miles.

There's the surging enthusiasm of the aficionados, too, who in high spirits have been spending a billion dollars a year on their machines, accessories, apparel, and related vacations, plus an estimated additional billion dollars for services contingent on this new way of enjoying snow.

THE SNARL INSTEAD OF THE HOWL

Where the winter sun never rises and the summer sun never sets, the snowmobile's snarl is becoming more common in many regions than the sled dog's howl. This is particularly noteworthy when you take into account that some trappers want to be buried with their huskies and malamutes because they never saw the hole their dog team couldn't pull them out of.

Only two decades after 225 of the first mass-produced recreational one- and-two-passenger snowmobiles were built and sold by Quebec's Bombardier, Ltd., snowmobiling has become an international sport with more than fifteen million participants.

It had a stay-safe aspect even at the start. The incentive driving Joseph-Armand Bombardier to design and construct the lightweight over-snow vehicles was the death of his oldest son from appendicitis after snowdrifts prevented medical assistance from arriving in time.

During the following decade, over a hundred manufacturers began marketing snowmobiles whose sales grew to five hundred thousand. Now, another decade later, some four million of the machines have reached the also explosively expanding network of man-made trails over which to ride them.

Snowmobiling and the long popular skating are similar. On skates you skim upon a ribbon of water. In snowmobiles in deep undisturbed snow, you really cruise atop compressed air.

THE SUBTLE HAZARD

In the farther places the major hazard lies in the reality that it's easier to snowmobile further in half an hour than, if the machine breaks down, to get back in the half a week it can take, especially alive.

However, the techniques considered in the chapters about camping, ice climbing, and cold-country adventuring can turn these potential disasters into sheer adventure. Once you realize even subconsciously that circumstances are such that you cannot afford to have a really decisive accident, such as letting a stalled snowmobile stop you, the probabilities shift markedly against any such mishap occurring.

Nowhere is this more evident than in the unpeopled places, where what may be a self-punishing, attention-getting, or responsibility-relieving misstep where help is at hand, now that you are on your own can be fatal. I guess that's how a lot of us keep going happily about life for years without trouble where, it's been said, the hand of man has seldom set foot.

KEEPING GOING IN DEEP SNOW

A deep fall of snow in cold country, with the wider tracks and the less overall weight, can set up what, for many, is the most pleasurable and relaxing snowmobiling of all. It's when you can lean back while the skis, kept high, swoop with uninterrupted lightness across the unmarked expanses.

Slackening that even pace, however, has the same effect as when you're riding on water skis behind a slowing launch. The snowmobile skis settle, too. They also have the same tendency to bury themselves when you lead forward.

Escaping a then entrapping drift can frequently be eased by getting out and freeing the skis, then reboarding as far back on the vehicle as you can so as to give the rear of the tracks increased traction. When the snow beneath them is packed by rocking and the power accelerated gradually, you generally can pull free without a wrenched back or strained muscle.

If this is not enough to get loose, there's always again clearing the tracks of snow, then compacting what's underneath and ahead with your feet. Trying to help matters along by packing branches and other foreign material under the tracks or by pushing the vehicle by the handlebars while you give it the gas, are unduly risky except as last-ditch resorts.

CONTROL

Until increasing fatigue gets in the way, kneeling, or for shorter periods standing, gives you surer control of any hazards ahead and roughnesses beneath. Both positions, besides establishing better visibility, make easier the swift balanced shifting of weight that keeps the track flat.

When a sharp rise intervenes, there's also then the increased freedom to lean forward while you're building speed for that last-moment tilt which will keep you from dead-centering on top. You're less likely to falter going up the steeper hills when, after an accelerated approach, you can hunch well ahead to concentrate all moveable weight on the skis and the front of the track.

Downhill, the sitting position affords steadier handling. Then, as whenever you're underway, the feet should never extend beyond the protection of the running boards, which should be kept free of slippery ice and snow.

SAFETY MARGIN

Going down slopes on a slant gives you safer charge, up to the point where steepness makes rolling too likely. Even then, soft snow is often sufficiently deep to angle into on the uphill side enough to keep level. The danger at such times is that unexpected ice or crust can mean going over sideways. When a situation is too doubtful, you may do better coming straight down.

Braking brings its own problems, almost all of which can be avoided if you extend your range of awareness. The result, when implemented to some extent by compression, also prolongs brake efficiency.

As for turning agility, this is determined primarily by the weight on the skis. Also important are the size of the track they make and the angle at which during the turn their bearing surface lies. At work will be simple friction, and the skill with which it is used.

KILLING THE MOTOR IN A PINCH

Making sure the throttle is free before starting the motor becomes increasingly important as winter cold tightens its hold and any sticking tendency of the fuel control begins multiplying. With some machines the habit chilly mornings of just giving the throttle a quick pull, then holding it open until the motor catches, one dawn can leave you plumb afoot.

A way to save the day when a throttle cable jams or freezes on the trail is, when you can, to flip the ignition off in time or press a kill button. When an engine runs on regardless, being ready to choke the carburetor, if necessary by blocking its opening with your palm, can usually mean getting out of more outdoor trouble.

TRANSPORT WITH LESS TROUBLE

When access to the luring trails means trailering the snowmobile first, the safest way to start is by riding it to the back of the carrier cautiously and under power, then switching the engine off and getting out.

When the trailer is two-wheeled, see next that its bed is tilted. Then when there's a winch, it's just a matter of hooking its cable to the machine and gradually reeling it aboard. Otherwise, most of us pull the snowmobile onto the trailer by hand, if we're lucky with the help of somebody else; then cover it with a tarpaulin or such, and take the time to snug everything down, front and rear, staunchly enough to hold. Unloading safely means pulling, or when necessary lifting, the vehicle off by hand.

There's less exposure to strain with a pickup truck when you can back it into a snowbank each time.

TOWING WITH MINIMAL RISK

Even when the most dependable reflector-equipped tow-sled is loaded so as to maintain the lowest practical center of gravity, a rigid tow bar sets the way for hauling it safely behind the snowmobile.

Any sled passengers increase the advisability of moderate speeds and smoother routes. When crossing roads, it is only reasonable for any human cargo to ease off the hauled vehicle and walk.

When towing another snowmobile, the first step well may be removing its drive belt. Then you will probably tie an end of an adequate towline to the loop in one of its skis, run the rope through the towing vehicle's trail hitch or rear bumper, bring it back to the second machine's other ski loop, and tie off securely.

Remember that braking, except when going uphill, ordinarily will leave the snowmobile behind still coasting. When everything's over, however uneventfully, it is still sound practice to check ski alignment.

To tow a toboggan or ordinary sled safely, you have to be awfully careful.

THE TROUBLE WITH ICE

The only practical difference between breaking through ice when snowmobiling or when skating is that breaking through when snowmobiling often occurs on ice strong enough to support you if you were afoot.

If you venture onto a frozen river or lake without knowing what to expect, you'll be better off figuring on probably going through and being ready for getting out.

Sometimes a snowmobile will settle slowly enough and in a compact enough space that there will be sufficient opportunity to step free. A lot of the time, though, such misadventures don't happen in slow motion.

Even stopping in time when open water suddenly appears ahead can quickly set up its own problems unless you're traveling well enough under control to make gradual braking effective. Otherwise, though leaning into an emergency turn, you're apt to spin out, off, and forward, often with enough momentum to slide the rest of the way into the liquid black cold.

Chapter 9

The Zest in Safe Reloading

The pleasure of each outdoor encounter has three parts: the enjoyment of getting ready, the pleasure of remembering, and the event itself.

Not the least is the anticipation, with its purposeful hours of exploring counters and catalogs, and the promise of adding and occasionally even subtracting, on odd margins and crowded envelope backs, notes having to do with that indispensable equipment that is difficult to come by.

Adding particular savor for more than a million shooters to blizzard-scuffed days and sleet-drumming evenings, when even the wildlife is holing up, is the personal control and the economy-extending satisfaction of reloading their own cartridges and shells.

Among the more demanding enthusiasts, the challenge of accuracy and precision approaches the scientific, giving even more purpose to those winter hours indoors.

STORING RELOADING COMPONENTS SAFELY

Modern smokeless powders create no explosion hazards despite some uninformed mistrust. Less flammable than many household polishes and cleaning fluids, they do not even set up fire danger if adequately stored.

Propellant powder can be safely kept in original or shipping containers inside wooden cabinets, locked or not depending on your situation. The heat-conducting properties of metal facilities, however, make storage in these more vulnerable in the event of a general fire.

In avoiding higher risk areas, though, the propellent powders should not be relegated to damp cellars or the periodic overheat of most unventilated attics, both of which eventually bring about deterioration.

Similar good sense applies to primer storing. In addition, the National Fire Prevention Association suggests that no more than ten thousand primers be kept in the home and no more than twenty-five thousand be transported at any one time in a car or boat. Anyone involved with any large quantity of primers and powder also will do well to check fire insurance coverage, along with local and state fire regulations which in some instances have quantity and storage provisions.

WHITE SMOKE AND BLACK POWDER

The shooters of the muzzleloaders get closer to the frontier days, partly because the more basically primitive powders they use enjoin a lot more personal attention than the smokeless propellents, including the good sense of limiting stores in today's living quarters to what can be used in a short time.

Because of its classification in any amount as a Class A Low Explosive, black powder presently comes under varying civil controls and fire prevention regulations, as well as occasional modifications of some fire insurance policies. Maintenance of reasonable supplies for use in sporting arms ammunition is not ordinarily impaired, however.

No gunpowder other than black powder or the more recently developed replica black powder in any of its four granulations, marketed as Pynadex, is safe to shoot in a muzzleloader—whether matchlock, wheellock, or flintlock.

During the more than 500 years of muzzleloaders, not even the invention of the percussion cap ignition system early in the nineteenth century has been able to dislodge the flintlocks among the single-shot devotees who, sensing more and more that initiative is being diminished by technology, still hunt with them in every state.

THE INIMITABLE MUZZLELOADERS

Before getting the feel of firing your own muzzleloader, it's well each time to be especially sure it is not overcharged and that the ball is firmly seated.

A good idea is to get in the habit of treating misfires and failures to fire with extreme care, keeping the barrel pointed in a safe direction while you wait at least one full minute before repriming.

There's the realistic precaution, too, of keeping either smokers or yourself somewhere else while loading, shooting, and even handling the adrenaline-stirring black powder explosives.

PRECAUTIONS WITH PIONEER WEAPONRY

Before loading and firing any antique gun, as contrasted to a working modern replica, it is only reasonable to have a dependable gunsmith certify it is in shootable condition.

If the weapon is a percussion lock, never carry it with the hammer at full cock. You'll see old-timers continuing to hunt with these guns loaded and capped but still on half cock.

With cap and ball revolvers, a lubricant placed pioneer fashion in the chamber mouth over the ball after loading or a modern waxed felt revolver wad imposed between powder and ball are insider ways of sealing the chamber to deter multiple discharges.

II

SPRING

Whether it be on the mountains in the north, or the plains in the south, or in the shelter of the foothills, spring comes in a night. It is winter when you go to bed one night and when you awaken next morning it is spring, and round you all nature is rejoicing in anticipation of the pleasures that lie ahead, plentiful food, warmth, and the reproduction of life.

Jim Corbett

Chapter 10

Fishing Again Tomorrow

High waves sometimes sweep unexpecting saltwater anglers from coastal ledges and rocks, especially along the steeper Pacific shore where mountains slant into the ocean. Anyone fishing or crossing such exposed areas will do well to keep watching out to sea for any approaching crest.

Then wherever it's reasonable to be, predetermining a realistic escape route should leave enough time to scramble or climb to safety. Being less concerned with the incoming tide than with the swirl of the pool below can mean, if nothing worse, lost gear.

If engulfed, however icily, staying alive can depend on managing not to be smashed or torn from a makeshift handhold during the next violent moments.

When storm or fog smothers your chance of spotting far enough out the towering advance of such swells, these jagged stretches of coastline are better shunned entirely or, at the least, traversed from already identified graspable spur to jutting outcrop to other promise of sanctuary.

WHERE FISHING SAFETY BEGINS

More than 63 million Americans, more than half of the multiplying horde now participating in the country's outdoor recreation, join yearly in the relaxation of sport fishing. A third of today's fishing licenses belong to women. There are no records of the additional millions of both sexes over sixty-five and under seventeen who in most states legally fish for free.

The number of young people under seventeen presently fishing is estimated to be twenty million, which suggests the family is where most of this national sport's safety basics are still learned. Seventy-five percent of the present crop of American anglers began to fish before they were twelve years old. Most were introduced by a parent or other close relative to the soul-satisfying atavism, an inheritance from our earliest ancestors who were catching fish long before they found fire to cook their finny booty.

GETTING UNHOOKED

An everyday part of sport fishing safety is keeping from being hooked and, when unsuccessful, in getting unhooked with the least damage.

When a fishhook becomes embedded beyond its barb, additional injury can frequently be reduced by pushing it on through. Once the barb is exposed, this can be snipped off or otherwise detached and the hook smoothly withdrawn. Or the shank may be severed and the hook pulled backward the rest of the way free.

These methods make the pocketing of some small cutting implement, such as one of the special pliers designed for fishing, a doubly sound precaution.

Even such a small wound, because it is penetrating, is difficult to treat beyond washing the skin surface well with water and soap. This will usually be enough when tetanus immunity is current. Watching the area a few days in case of infection, which then can generally be stemmed before it has time to become dangerous, makes a safe outcome still more likely.

SIDESTEPPING TETANUS TROUBLE

Danger from tetanus, present everywhere when the skin is scratched or even scraped and especially threatening in puncture wounds where

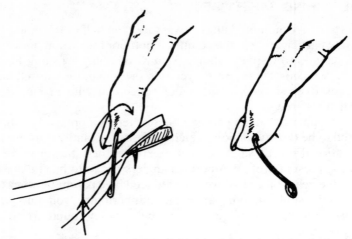

Figure 8. Once a fishhook becomes embedded in the skin beyond its barb, push it on through. When the barb appears, it can be snipped off and the hook withdrawn.

the air can't reach, should be eliminated by immunization before any serious fishing or, realistically, any other recreation outdoors.

If it hasn't been, a safeguard remaining will be administration of tetanus antitoxin at the time of the hurt or, when this happens in a remote area, within two or three days.

It is impractical to carry antitoxin in an emergency kit. You never know, anyway, when even the most trifling break in the skin is going to let in the deadly bacterium.

The passive immunity resulting from the injected antitoxin protects no more than six weeks and then with some risk—two reasons to stay immunized against these ever-present spores.

Immunization from tetanus usually takes only one injection, almost never more than two. Once immunity is established by the tetanus toxoid, which takes several months, no more than a booster shot ordinarily will be indicated after even severe injury for as long as the immunity is kept up.

No cure is known once lockjaw develops.

AFTER A DAY OF CASTING

Some of the feminine bait-and-fly-casting enthusiasts are troubled with swelling in their wrists at the end of a day with rod and reel in a stream or in the surf. This in turn brings on stiffening fingers, accompanied often by numbness, pain, tingling, and sometimes burning.

A few of these anglers arouse at night shaking their hands to wake them up. This movement massages fluid out of the extremities and is often relieving, inasmuch as the trouble involves pressure on the median nerve, frequently in association with fluid retention during the menopausal period.

The Carpal Tunnel Syndrome can in many instances be aborted by anti-inflammatory medicines, diuretics, sometimes wrist splints, and exercises to mobilize the fingers. A more extreme resort is surgery.

PNEUMATIC POSSIBILITIES

Inflatable boats are more safely opening some of the remoter fishing waters, although their fabrics are bringing their own problems.

A few minor precautions may well be taken when using fishhooks, knives, and gaffs. However, as Don Hubbard, a retired naval aviator and commander, puts it in *The Complete Book of Inflatable Boats,* the same safeguards are warranted when using these items around a puncturable human being.

If your equipment is properly stowed aboard, both your personal and boating problems should be few. If you scatter loose fishhooks around the craft, they are as apt to get in a foot as in a hull tube. A large piece of cork can neutralize the point of a gaff, unless you find bringing a collapsible net handier. Knives which can be folded or sheathed will cut bait and dress fish almost as well as the rest.

When the hook you're pulling in happens to snag the slightly protruding lower edge of a patch or seam, if you hold up long enough to ease it out, that generally will be all there is to it. If not, the first thing is to find the leak so you can stop or slow the loss of air pressure.

A small puncture at or above the waterline generally can be controlled by a finger, less so usually with a wide strip of tape, long enough to run in to shore. If the boat softens appreciably while you're attempting to locate the trouble, it's ordinarily a simple thing to use your pump long enough to put in sufficient air.

Even with a serious rip, trapped air and the support of adjacent chambers will almost always keep the tube partially inflated until you can get out of difficulty. Truly disabling damage to a good inflatable is rare, unless you have a psychopath aboard.

"On hard-shelled boats, high impact damage which holes the hull will mean swamping and clinging to an almost submerged boat," says Commander Hubbard. "I'll take my chances on an inflatable any time."

THE BUOYANCY QUANDARY

Waders with buoyancy chambers now make it easier for the fisherman who looses footing, or steps into deep water, to maneuver out of trouble.

The conventional waders, however, have seldom been as dangerous as many have feared. The idea that someone falling in them will be pulled to the river bottom, especially when wearing heavy clothing, is not borne out by experience.

When someone takes a header beyond his depth while dressed in traditional garb, including the usual waders, it's true that air will generally be trapped in the waders. However, upon relaxing the angler will surface. His feet will emerge first. All he has to do to keep the air trapped is ease up his head, his body relax horizontally, and allow his legs to sag at the knees. He'll then be able to float comfortably on his back and assess the situation before making his next move, which probably will be to paddle carefully to shore.

If the fisherman steps into the deep water, air will be driven out of his boots. But then enough can be expected to stay caught in his shirt and jacket to return him to the surface, and let him float easily there on his back while stroking toward the shallows.

Chapter 11

Going Camping and Coming Back

Spring brings its urge to go deep into the undisturbed open places, where verdancy is spreading across the treetops and the ground below like green fire, and where a lone camp and what goes with it are best. Usually this is well in from the roads where the less particular don't take the energy, imagination, or time to go and where, consequently, you'll be safest.

There the day is apt to come when you have not pulled yourself loose before dark, at best a disproportionately hazardous time to travel the woods when you don't have to, and when a comfortable spike camp by a rollicking brook beckons all the more luringly.

Here, when you're far enough back to manage it, a campfire is always companionable, and it can light things while you gather the fuel to keep it going. Building a long fire and lying between it and a log is hard to equal mild nights, when it's most pleasant sleeping on pine needles under the stars.

In less clement weather, sitting relaxed against the trunk of a small fir or spruce in a niche you've made by stripping away a few of its boughs, especially with a campfire breaking away to coals in front, is snugger. Or just gather several armfuls of conifer braches, slant them

Figure 9. One seldom feels more attuned to the outdoors than while drowsing between a fire and heat-reflecting log.

against a fallen tree or a pole you stretch perhaps between two saplings, and enjoy the unforgettable luxury of your own private lean-to.

When cold is a problem, halfway up the lee side of a wooded slope will ordinarily be warmer than either above or below.

During hot weather in hilly country, its lowlands when cut by a stream are more agreeable, in part because air currents tend to discourage insects. Clutter or scars left by high water can warn of where to camp beyond the reach of any flooding, whose suddenness is an extreme hazard along the streambeds and dry low courses in desert reaches.

IN ANY EVENT

Such bivouacs will linger in your memory as the high points of camping and foraging, and of a great many other things. They will, that is, for those who go through the out-of-doors interested. If you are uninterested, you will see nothing but the traveled way.

In any event, as the Hudson's Bay Company, with the experience of three centuries in this continent's farther places, still cautions its far-flung fur traders, "If for any reason you leave an emergency camp, even if only for a short period, leave a note in an obvious place stating in detail your plans and where you're going."

Figure 10A. What is snugger than an aromatic niche made by stripping a few boughs from a spruce or fir, when it's warmed by a campfire in front?

Figure 10B. Or just gather a few armfuls of conifer boughs, slant them against a pole laid between two trees, and enjoy the luxury of your own lean-to.

THE FREEDOM IN KNOWING WHERE YOU ARE

As long as you remain uneasy about getting lost, you are not going to feel the very real satisfaction and the unequaled freedom of roaming unworried on your own.

You may sense such liberation all of a sudden one day, when unexpectedly it comes over you that the solution is just to stay found. This simple answer, you may soon discover, is also the easiest and by far the most intriguing. You merely keep marking on a map exactly where you go. If you don't have a map, you draw one on some handy paper as you go along. Bringing this map up to date about every ten minutes, or whenever you change direction, is the surest way to keep track of your whereabouts, at least for a while.

The wiliest old mountain man or woodsman does exactly the same thing whether he realizes it or not. His map is in his head, that's all. You will be using mental maps, too, once you get the feel of it all.

WHICH NORTH?

A compass, the simpler the better, will help. Later one more precise and detailed may be more interesting. There are many ways to tell direction without a compass, just as there are numerous ways to start a campfire without a match, but both compasses and matches save a lot of time.

If you hold or set a magnetic compass level and away from attracting metal in the United States and Canada, it will point north; magnetic north, that is, a shifting point below and slightly east of the north pole. This difference may be important when you're using a printed map, many of which show what this declination is in your general vicinity.

If your map doesn't, during the first clear night mark the direction to the North Star, which stays within about one degree of true north. When it's daylight, compare your line to the direction the compass is pointing. This difference is the declination, what you allow for on a printed map. When you just travel by your compass's magnetic north when you leave camp, all you have to do is come back in the opposite direction.

The North Star is most easily located with the help of the Big Dipper. Just follow an imaginary line joining the two stars forming the Big Dipper's outer edge from bottom to top about five of its own lengths farther. There, Polaris's solitary beacon shines, apart from the other some two thousand visible stars, reassuringly above the northernmost part of the earth.

THE BEST WAY OF GETTING THERE

Suppose your camp is on a river, at the base of a mountain range, or along another such long landmark. This sort of boundary whenever possible you soon come to seek for a campsite or starting place.

Let us assume that this stretches east to west, and that today the spring bear-hunting season is opening. If you hunt north of this line in the morning, hunting south in the afternoon will bring you back to the line. But if this is unfamiliar country, is camp right or left?

If the next day when again hunting northward you keep sufficient track on your little map of where you go, you will be able to head back to one definite side of your camp. Aiming just a few degrees to one side, for example north northwest, will be sufficient. Then upon reaching the long boundary, you'll know which way to follow it.

This technique can be reversed to locate a trail heading directly away. Say this is a long tote road, running south from another area and stopping about a mile due north of your camp on the east-west boundary. Then it will just be a matter of angling a bit either side of due north, for about a mile and a half. You can then turn directly toward the tote road, as certain as one may be of anything that it stretches broadside nearby.

Distance in the wilds is most easily measured by time. If you hunt north for three hours, hunting south at about the same pace for about another three hours will get you back.

DENSE FLAT COUNTRY

Getting back to camp in dense flat country just takes more work. What you need is a larger mark to aim at. So the first day everyone, even if your *we* is *me,* begins blazing two lines of trees, their lengths depending on the situation.

With your camp in the center the blazes can extend, for example, north and south and from east to west. Then it will be only a matter of keeping close enough track of your whereabouts to be sure of heading back into this target.

Nicking each tree higher on the side nearer camp can make returning there, while the evening's stew is still hot in your buried Dutch oven, even easier.

IF YOUR COMPASS IS LOST

The sun is another means of determining direction. The moon, too, moves from east to west.

Moss does grow best on the shady north side of trees in the open, although it may be important, depending where you are, not to confuse moss with lichens, some of which thrive on the trunk's sunniest parts.

Then there is the prevailing wind. Even when it is not blowing, the signs of it remain. In open country, away from such diverting landmarks as ravines and hills, sand and snow build up on the downwind sides of rocks, knolls, banks, and the willow clumps. Drifts are lower and narrower to windward.

Along Canada's great eastern barrens and semibarrens, the prevailing wind slants trees toward the southwest, and in winter whisks snow from the bottoms of drifts, giving them the appearance of anvils. These point northwest.

Everywhere, old snow is more granular on the southern side of ridges and hills than on the northern side.

Poplar, alder, and willow are persuaded by the sun into southward tilts, where prevailing wind doesn't influence them in a different direction. The tops of hemlock, pine, and similar conifers tip naturally toward the sun-rising east. These softwoods tend to be bushiest on the south, particularly when growing in unlimited sunlight.

Age rings in the standing stumps of trees which grew long enough unshaded for the south to prevail as their sunniest side are widest along their southern arcs.

Ants seek the warm south sides of trees and rocks when they build their hills. Vegetation grows smaller and denser on southern slopes, larger and more apart along the northern exposures.

Mountain men often keep oriented in big country by watersheds, although some get in trouble along the Continental Divide, where in places only a few feet separate water courses that on the East ultimately reach the Atlantic Ocean and on the West drain into the Pacific.

Chapter 12

When Your Yacht is Your Canoe

Wind carries the danger in canoeing, both in sudden savagery and in the big seas it blows up when high and steady. Rain is just disagreeable. Its combination with wind in squalls, however, builds into extreme hazard. Worst are cold fronts, often appearing as long black lines.

Thunderstorms sometimes churn mile-a-minute gusts. Although any peril from lightning is an overrated part, this is greater on water than on land. The safest tactic when caught out during an electrical disturbance is to beach the canoe among uniformly high trees, and for shelter perhaps overturning it and getting beneath. Single trees standing tall in the open particularly should be avoided.

The Southwest's man-made lakes hold special peril in that thermals born of desert heat swoop across many in bursts which, although too short-lived to drive up high combers, may hit the craft at ninety miles per hour. The seasoned canoeist, alerted by oncoming streaks on the water, gets his or her weight as low as possible and heads into the blow.

THE HAZARDS OF HYDRAULICS

Although more visible than the dangers of cold-water immersion, the insidious hazards of hydraulics are even more often underrated. Yet when you are wading a stream with a ten-mile-per-hour current, a weight of more than three hundred pounds is shoving against your legs. A canoe immersed there will have a thrust of more than three tons.

If your canoe goes over in fast water, staying safe can depend on keeping upstream of it. When spilled ahead, the most prudent action will ordinarily be to duck or dodge when it careens by, then if possible to grab the stern and hang on as the craft rides through the remaining rapids, as if you were grasping the tail of a swimming horse.

Because of its then greater depth, the canoe handled this way will seek the deeper water, usually plunging untouched through tight reaches with amazing alacrity.

If left canoeless, your safest way through a welter of cascades and rocks will be on your back feet first, treading water until coming to a quiet reach and sanctuary.

STAYING AFLOAT SAFELY

Personal flotation provisions go along with reasonable canoeing, even when several craft are traveling together. The same white water or squall that gets one in trouble is apt to be setting up enough difficulties for the others to delay, at best, any assistance in an emergency. Then not even the ability to swim well can be counted on as an adequate substitute for a life vest or better.

All-purpose jackets with intrinsic buoyancy, in company with inflatable vests and their ilk, are bettering the safety statistics. They still show, though, a greater number of drownings occurring among good swimmers than there should be.

The more specialized, bright-colored preservers that go over the neck and extend down the front are the soundest choices in rugged going. Floatable cushions remain at the low end of the safety scale, partly because of their inclination to bob out of reach in current and breeze.

For serious canoeing, the personal flotation device should be individually selected to fit. As well as assuring comfort and free movement both in and out of the water, it should be easily donned and doffed. Preferably, it will be highly visible. Especially when rough rapids may be in the future, a flotation device should have the positive-righting construction and the buoyancy to keep the head and neck of even someone unconscious safely above the surface. Ideally, it will be worn.

PADDLING STABILITY

Taking what has become the accepted position in a canoe, on a seat, puts the center of gravity higher than in any other popular boat. The craft, especially with its roundness, can roll over easily.

Paddling while sitting or kneeling on the canoe bottom, as the Indian designers intended, shifts this critical gravity center well below the midpoint of the roll.

When winds rise and seas roughen, stability can be dramatically increased in a moment just by moving down from the seat. An even wider safety margin can be assured by also always centering the weight and load whenever possible, leaving bow and stern light, free to rise in the waves and, if necessary, to be spun toward smoother water.

The kneeling position, the one still found most effective by many modern voyageurs, can soon be maintained comfortably for hours with the help of padding as nearby as a flotation cushion or folded jacket, particularly when there's a thwart against which to rest the hips.

THE STAY-SAFE FORMULA

The basic formula in the outdoor science of staying safe, hope for the best but prepare for the worst, is particularly applicable when canoeing.

It is also a reason for gaining at the beginning more than ordinary familiarity with the craft's on-board capabilities. Learning to paddle standing can set up safer last-moment checks of the likelier channels through nearing rapids. Even paddling astride the gunwales can overcome, before it matters, undue apprehension about capsizing.

THE TIME FOR PRECAUTION

The ancient blue water adage, that the time to take precaution for the safety of the ship is when you have time to take precaution, holds especially with the relatively light and fragile canoe.

One thing it points up is that overloading, the most common cause of all small boat accidents, can be unwarrantably hazardous when canoeing away from the sanctuary of the almost always more safely skirted shore.

Heading across large lakes in a canoe under any circumstances involves risks best avoided whenever possible. On northern waters the custom is to follow strings of islands.

Without the experience it is difficult to realize how frail a canoe

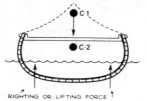

LOW CENTER OF GRAVITY
KNEELING — PADDLING
C-1 IS CENTER OF GRAVITY
C-2 IS THE CENTER OF LATERAL STABILITY
SINCE THE TWO ARE CLOSE IT IS HARD TO CAPSIZE
BOAT.

C-1

C-2

RIGHTING OR LIFTING FORCE

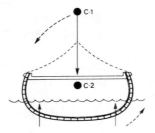

C-1

C-2

HIGH CENTER OF GRAVITY
WHEN MAN SITS ON SEAT
CENTER OF GRAVITY RISES,
DISTANCE OF TURNING
"FULCRUM" IS GREATER.

WITH LONGER "FULCRUM"
IT IS EASIER TO GET
GRAVITY PULL OVERCOMING
CENTER OF STABILITIES
RIGHTING ACTION.

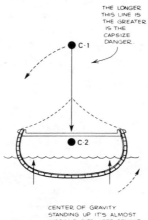

THE LONGER
THIS LINE IS
THE GREATER
IS THE
CAPSIZE
DANGER.

C-1

C-2

CENTER OF GRAVITY
STANDING UP IT'S ALMOST
IMPOSSIBLE TO KEEP CENTER
OF STABILITY IN LINE WITH
CENTER OF GRAVITY.

Figure 11. Kneeling or sitting on the canoe bottom, as Indian designers intended, keeps the critical gravity center well below where the craft's roll is located.

becomes in big water when the wind starts to blow. With the usual open canoe packed for a two-week journey, trouble starts when the crests are no more than a foot high. Quickly there's a bailing situation, at the same time full attention is needed just to handle the craft.

When caught away from shelter in waves that threaten swamping, your best offensive often becomes turning and running before the seas. Then, with the canoe's increased speed keeping its stern longer in each swell, there's more chance for the bow to lift, instead of burrowing into the comber ahead.

OVERBOARD AND OVERTURNED

What can save a situation is when it becomes almost second nature to right an overturned canoe by pressing down on a gunwale until the craft slowly rolls upright, then easing back aboard carefully enough not to upset it again, sitting or kneeling on the bottom, and paddling ashore with just the hands if necessary.

There is also the rarer crisis when occupants are lurched overboard from a rolling canoe which, empty, corrects itself and floats free. Especially in wind and white water, your future may hinge on reacting swiftly enough to capture the vehicle before it swerves beyond reach. Afterward, if land is close, the canoe often can best be swum to shore.

When haven is more remote and a companion is also overboard, what commonly works begins with one person steadying either the bow or stern with both hands. The other person, gripping a gunwale amidships, usually can then kick himself flat in the water at right angles to the sides and pull himself forward into the craft. There, grabbing the farther gunwale, he should be able to heave his body across both, upon which jackknifing fully aboard becomes easy. Then, a hand on each gunwale, he can balance the canoe while the other person becomes a passenger in the same manner.

If the empty canoe has shipped considerable water, often it must first be lightened. The swimmers generally only need to press one end low enough for part of the burden to flow out, then move amidships and rock the craft to slosh out most of the remainder. If waves are running, though, as much water will probably tend to splash in as you are able to urge out.

LETTING WIND EASE YOUR WAY

With sailing becoming an increasingly popular adjunct to canoeing with pole and paddle, Grumman, whose sleek aluminum canoes first

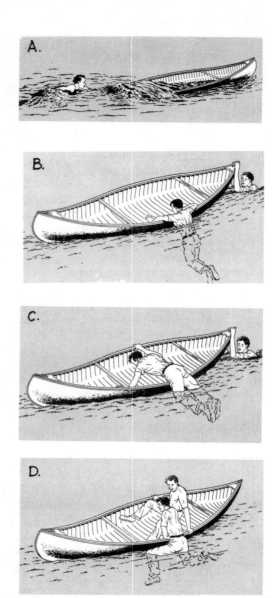

Figure 12. (A) When two are overboard and the canoe rights itself after shipping water, empty it by first pressing one end far enough down to let the bulk flow out. (B) To reboard, one of you steadies the bow or stern, while the other grasps a gunwale amidships. (C) Then kicking himself flat on the surface, he heaves his body across both gunwales. (D) Bracing himself in the center, the boarded passenger balances the craft while the other swimmer boards the same way.

overtook and soon outnumbered this country's canvas-covereds, once more has an answer. Its present models are factory-prepared for all three sail rigs: the forty-five-square-foot lateen, the sixty-five-square-foot gunter, and the new fifty-five-square-foot American Canoe Association Class C sail rigging.

Each comes with aluminum mast and boom, sail, leeboards and spreader bar, rudder and adapter, and all the lines. As for the owner of an earlier Grumman who also has a screwdriver and pair of pliers, this capability is a matter of specifying to the company that canoe's size and model number.

Canadians, despite marine aluminum's ascendency elsewhere on this continent's waters, still continue paddling, poling, and portaging the more traditional and beautiful of the canvas old-liners, in the ratio of four out of every five transactions. When you have canoed in one in the Canadian wilds, as I've done from coast to coast, it is easy to appreciate why.

The Chestnuts, with which the oldest of the modern manufacturers overcame the wooden canoe's weighty tendency to soak up water by adding in the late 1800s a canvas cover, range increasingly from the southern provinces to the Arctic. Old Town's cedar-strips, whose design is almost unchanged since the turn of the century but whose exterior cloth is now fiberglass, often still travel in line.

One of the new-generation canoes south of the border is Coleman's stealthy and nearly indestructible RAM-X model, its space-age hull formulated especially for the sport from an ultrahigh molecular weight polyethylene, which has proved durable so far at all streamside temperatures.

THE CHOICE OF SECURITY

A disabled canoe, when there's a choice, offers greater security than no canoe. Not only can it be spotted more quickly than you, but it's then more readily recognized as being in trouble.

Meantime, it generally provides a way to get mostly, if not entirely, out of the water. If you're only swamped or capsized, it's usually a means to get out of the difficulty entirely.

Rarely should anyone leave a disabled canoe, especially in back country, and swim for shore even though this may seem absurdly near. The safer procedure is usually to swim the canoe to land.

As for being stranded alone there awhile, it is only before one no longer is a stranger to the joy of solitude that the solitary places are ever distressing. Afterward, they are eloquently exquisite.

Chapter 13

The Greatest Living Hazards

Far more dangerous in the outdoors than any wild animal are the mosquitoes and black flies, so thick in scantily populated vastnesses of the United States and Canada that they can kill a full grown man or woman who is stranded, astray, or just camping there without adequate knowledge, gear, or ingenuity.

Some individuals are more attractive than others to the winged biters, the differences being physiological and occasionally emotional. What especially lures the mosquitoes, black flies, deer flies, pesky gnats, and the confounded rest to Homo sapiens and other mammals is the amount of carbon dioxide they emit.

Camouflage or camouflaged clothing can give protection from at least the horseflies, for the element most often arousing their attention is contrast. Shapes, sizes, and colors are secondary.

N. O. Morgan, research entomologist at the United States Department of Agriculture's Environmental Quality Institute in Maryland, has found the most effective trap for the salt-marsh greenhead horsefly to be a glossy black or dark blue drum or box device placed in clearings and on prominent rises, easily visible to low flying insects against the ground or sky. In Mississippi's woods where openings have dark backgrounds, the same traps painted white draw best.

"Unfortunately, biting flies respond to target movements," the entomologist adds, "and we are the targets. In our area the deerfly is a pest only if you walk near a bush where it rests. Normally, it actively seeks blood meals for about the last thirty minutes before sundown, whereas horseflies tend to feed all day.

"As far as chemical repellents go, we use an aerosol formulation of DEET (N, N-diethyl-meta-toluamide) with 71 to 75 percent active ingredients. This gives eight to ten hours of protection from most biting flies, provided it does not get washed off. The repellent is water soluble, so even light perspiration may reduce its effectiveness."

DEET

The most effective commercial repellents continue to be those based on DEET. I was involved, together with Col. Townsend Whelen, in its earliest field testing, and if only in self-defense, I've never stopped using it. The best protector available to the public I've ever found is Muskol Insect Repellent Lotion, which is 95 percent DEET. An American product bottled in Canada, where it has been available for the last two decades, it is now reaching stores in the United States. The home source is Muscol, Ltd., P.O. Box 644, Truro, Nova Scotia.

Deet is poisonous. It can cause brain damage to infants if used repeatedly on skin.

SMOKE, BARK, MOSS, MUD, AND NET

Since one of our ancestors built that first fire, smoke has helped everywhere to protect against the sometimes cloud-like swarms of mosquitoes and flies, as long as you can stay downwind of a smudge. On the move, if you've nothing more convenient, mud plastered over your exposed skin works.

Moss, sheaths of bark beneath each sock, even leaves buttoned inside your shirt can functionally reinforce inadequate clothing. The most heartening maneuver of all still is keeping whenever possible to wide shores, bare ridges, and the windy stretches.

The United States Department of Agriculture's Insects Affecting Man Laboratory in Gainesville, Florida, now has developed a repellent head and face protector for the Department of Defense, practical when you pitch your tent along waters at the top of the continent where the fish, which eat the little airborne menaces, grow largest.

WHEN A TURTLE ATTACKS

Snapping turtles and rattlesnakes (who at times strike without coiling and without even warning) are among the food sources available in the wilds if ever you are stranded, perhaps by spring floods.

The turtle's bite, while not poisonous, can mean a maimed foot or severed finger. The alligator snapper and even the common snapper are as fast as a bear's paw with their locking jaws. If a turtle ever clamps onto you or a companion, the best defense will be a reciprocally savage offense, going for a nostril or eye of the snapper with a sharp stick or, better, your knife.

WOOD, THORN, OR EVEN SNAKE

As for the practice more common a few years ago of treating rattlesnake bites, as well of those of the copperhead and water moccasin, by applying ice or cold compresses to the wound, there is evidence that this tends to localize the poison. A result, pinpointed by doctors, is tissue damage that in extreme cases has caused deformity and even required amputation.

SNAKEBITE KITS

Snakebite kits complete with simple instructions, such as Cutter's which takes up about as much room as a twelve-gauge shell, are credited with saving a significant number of lives when treatment is swift, a reason in snake country for keeping such aid always in a pocket.

When the particularly vulnerable leg, or any other such accessible part is bitten, tie a band 1½ inches above both bite and swelling, only tightly enough to restrict the flow of the lymph vessels. A tourniquet is unnecessary and can get you in worse trouble than most bites. Even the lace or whatever, tied as suggested, should be loosened a bit if the involved area numbs or becomes cold. Removing it for a minute about every ten minutes is recommended, then if you can reapplying it slightly higher, just beyond any extended swelling.

Meanwhile, clean the skin around the bite as well as is practical within a brief time. If you have a knife rather than the antiseptic blade in a commercial kit, sterilize the cutting edge in at least a match flame if you can.

Then make a quarter-inch cut through each fang mark, carefully enough to avoid tendons, arteries, large veins, and if possible nerves. Incisions should be kept entirely away from any prominently visible blood vessels.

With Cutter's and similar snakebite kits, squeeze the air out of each suction cup in turn and place one over each cut. It will hold better if the skin is damp. Steady, gentle suction is believed to be best. Don't pump. As any swelling progresses, make additional incisions and reapply the cups.

Or just suck and spit out blood and venom. A warmed bottle will, as it cools, provide one method of suction. If perhaps because of the position of the bite you can do nothing better, press and squeeze out the blood and any intermingled poison.

Much of the outcome depends on the size of the snake and the amount of venom injected. The time interval since the reptile last struck and emptied its poison sacs also is a factor.

Maybe it wasn't a poisonous snake at all. This revelation may come when you see a double row of tooth marks and no fang signs. Then the only treatment indicated is the same as for any puncture wound.

Thorns and pointed sticks are frequently mistaken for snakebites and blamed.

Chapter 14

Safe to Eat, Drink, and Use in a Pinch

Even the layer between the outer bark and trunk of the pine, spruce, and other conifers can be scraped or cut off and, as Indians did, enjoyed cooked or pleasantly raw.

Just drinking the strong dark tea with its pleasantly piquant Christmas tree flavor, which you can brew as you would grocery-store tea from these softwoods' green needles, will prevent and even cure scurvy which, unrecognized, has disabled and killed hundreds of people well into this century.

Why ever starve when stranded or astray in the wilderness, where overall no less than 120,000 varieties of wild plants alone are good to eat? Through ignorance and fastidiousness, a lot of individuals have starved.

While your strength is nearest its maximum is the time, during an emergency, to begin taking advantage of the bounty the unimproved places everywhere offer free for the gathering.

Beyond timberline in the North all vegetation except one mushroom is edible, although many of the lichens are better digested with their bitterness first soaked out.

Anywhere, a handbook on identifying wild edible plants may be reassuring to keep in a pocket. But never, ever, at any time, take unwarrantable chances.

MEAT ALONE CAN BE YOUR ANSWER

Fresh, adequately plump, not overcooked meat furnishes all the necessary food ingredients, even if you dine on nothing but sizzling rare steaks for a week, a month, or a decade.

The only danger common in getting along entirely on game is that an exclusive diet of the nearly fat-free hare or rabbit for more than a very few days brings on what is known in the Far North as rabbit-starvation, actually death from nephritis. Yet when fat is added, as it would be in ordinary circumstances by the butter and such in accompanying food, the meat is so desirable that the rabbit family remains North America's most hunted game.

SO CAN ONLY FISH

Freshly caught fish, not overcooked, will likewise keep any ordinarily healthy individual in top condition indefinitely, although to get enough calories you'll generally need a lot. With trout this can be ten to twelve pounds a day.

All the freshwater fish in America and Canada are wholesome. So are nearly all the saltwater fish that reach these shores, although the possibility remains that the occasional unfamiliar and strange looking poisonous fish may swim or drift this way from tropical waters.

THE TROUBLE CALLED TULAREMIA

Tularemia is infrequently found in some localities. A general safeguard is to take only those rabbit and hare which are lively and to all appearances healthy. A surer precaution is not to touch the animal with your bare hands until the meat is thoroughly cooked.

Rabbit is particularly easy to prepare even with gloves if you start by pinching up enough of the loose back skin to tear or slit open, then peel the hide off like a mitten, and finally detach the feet, head, and tail. The game can then be pulled open just below the ribs, and the entrails flung out with a single quick flip.

MAKING SURE OF SAFE WATER

There is also some tularemia in remote wilderness among beaver and muskrat, who when upstream can infect the drinking water below.

The safest principle is to assume all water is impure until it is proved otherwise. Even long-used wells are found still infecting present users with unsuspected tularemia and other undesirables, as they have earlier generations.

The surest way to purify water for your personal use, which includes any for brushing the teeth or for cooking when high heat is not a factor, is to boil it five minutes at sea level and another one minute for each added thousand feet of elevation.

Halazone has long been relied upon to purify small amounts of drinking water. Leave two of the tiny pills in a covered quart of water for half an hour. Both the amount of fresh halazone and the time are advisably doubled when the water is muddy or particularly questionable.

Similarly used iodine tablets, such as the Globeline also procurable along with its simple directions from sporting good stores and pharmacies, are effective in the semitropical and tropical regions where chlorine, halazone's active ingredient, cannot be depended on to do the job.

Eight drops of the less expensive and often handier 2½ percent tincture of iodine that is reasonably fresh can purify a quart of water in ten minutes, although when this is mountain-stream cold, twice that time will be safer.

The suggestion occasionally heard, usually from the drinker, that a high-proof alcoholic beverage will purify accompanying water and ice is based on nothing more substantial than, at best, hope.

FRESHWATER AND SALT

Safety some thirsty occasion may lie in knowing that sea ice loses its salinity so rapidly that it becomes fresh by the end of its first summer.

Likewise significant, in hotter climates, may be the knowledge that cramping brought on by loss of body salt in perspiration will disappear when replaced as by the salt in the usual meals.

During vigorous outdoor recreation, the convenient salt tablets are frequently included with the drinking water. Depending on salt tablets for very long, however, can delay heat acclimatization. Again, generally a judicious amount of salt in the diet is more than sufficient.

WHEN OUTDOOR ACTIVITY IS STRENUOUS

Strenuous activity during one of the more sweltering days, especially when the sun is oppressive, can cause the loss of body fluid equivalent to between 3 percent and 5 percent of an individual's total weight. This is the reason heat stroke annually kills football players needlessly during pre-season practice, a throwback to some of our youths when a coach believed that any more water than enough of a sip to moisten the throat would slow us down, if not make us sick.

Everywhere when body fluid gets below its optimum level, water remains the best known replacement. You can need to drink beyond perceived thirst, however, since this natural mechanism may cut off prematurely when fluid replenishment is as much as 50 percent short.

SAFETY KIT

If more than half a day away from civilization and doctors, a small and simple safety kit is a practical item to have along, when it is accompanied by reasonable knowledge about how to use it. Anything for which your experience indicates a probable need, and certainly that which your physician recommends, may well be among its contents.

Besides a bit of some concentrated food, mainly for reassurance if ever the outlook seems bleak, this kit may include a prescribed stimulant to be used only in a crisis when you or someone else may require extra sustained energy in a hurry. For such an emergency I've long carried several dexedrine sulfate tablets that a close friend, Thomas J. Gray, M.D., suggested because of his own experience in getting himself and others out of tight remote situations.

Ordinarily several little self-mixed and foil-wrapped packets of sugar and instant coffee will suffice. Before heading out, you can prepare these yourself, as they are better relatively fresh. Wrap separately enough for your usual steaming cup, although you'll keep these for dissolving in your mouth on the go when you need a quick energy boost.

BLISTERING ATTACK

Small adhesive bandages with plain nonmedicated gauze pads and the better adhering plastic tape can help to solve such everyday problems as tender spots on heels and toes before they blister. Afterwards, such adhesive pads can prevent futher friction until the area has time to heal.

Covering a blistered heel directly with tape shuts out ventilation and keeps the region moist and soft, with lessened chance to toughen. If the skin is already broken, infection then has all the more chance to develop.

ASPIRIN IS ASPIRIN *fresh !*

The only variant among aspirin, a minor one of time needed for absorption, appears among the tablet preparations as a result of different processing. Aspirin's therapeutic efficacy, however, is dependent on its age which, in company with air and moisture, sets up chemical breakdown. With dating now required on all drugs, it's simpler to stay equipped with a fresh supply.

Aspirin, being anti-inflammatory, can help bring down swelling which is interfering with the mechanical action of a knee, ankle, wrist, or shoulder. At the same time it can ease the discomfort, both directly and indirectly.

"It is the swelling and inflammation which cause pressure on nerve endings," says Dr. Julius M. Kowelski, medical advisor on the staff of the Outdoor Writers Association of America. "This, in turn, initiates pain."

Aspirin also reduces fever, in addition to having enough mildly analgesic power to subdue the ordinary headache. Some doctors suggest that when a common headache is slow in responding, a way out may be to alternate aspirin and acetaminophen, also known by the trade name Tylenol. Acetaminophen is chemically similar to aspirin, but a separate and compatible medicine not cumulative in the body, which also does not subdue inflammation. The headache routine indicated by these physicians is aspirin, then in two hours acetaminophen, aspirin again two hours later, and so on within the recommended dosages.

SAVING YOURSELF FROM CHOKING

When you're boiling the noonday kettle alone over a solitary campfire, there is always the chance you may choke on a kabob and be unable to breathe.

Dr. Henry J. Heimlich, a professor of Xavier University, suggests this maneuver may get you out of trouble: Hold a fist just below your ribs, slightly above your navel. Grasp this fist with the other hand. Press it forcefully into your abdomen with quick, hard, upward thrusts until the object is ejected and your airway cleared. Or throw yourself over a log, so as to exert sudden pressure in the same midabdominal area. (The Heimlich Maneuver is considered in detail in Chapter 19.)

Self inflicted Hemlock maneuvre.

Chapter 15

Space, Ice, and Snow

On springtime climbs up into lingering ice and snow, adequate clothing gives you not only comfort and the satisfaction of capability, but also the relaxing assurance that goes with staying safe.

Just having rubber soles, the only thing that is nearly indispensable on rock ascents, is no longer enough where slipping on a slope as apparently innocent as a calendar picture can mean serious injury or worse. The same end results lie in wait for anyone caught too lightly dressed in the deepening cold or blizzard that among the tall peaks often takes over a May day. Especially along the West Coast, where glacier-topped mountains slant up from balmy coastland cities, climbers for no better reason than proximity often make themselves the targets of rescue expeditions on heights which sometimes have lulled them by a lifetime of really only windowed familiarity. More than a quarter of the state of Washington's reported mountain accidents end fatally.

Yet low-temperature clothing considerations, within the limits expanded by the dramatic suddenness and severity of high altitude weather, are similar in ice and snow climbing to those of adventuring in such climatic conditions everywhere. The beginner may choose to borrow or rent the special gear in which to head up. But he or she can never rely on starting out short and coming back, especially erect.

Here even an unanticipated shower may freeze in verglas's slippery invisibility. This alone can mean, if nothing sooner, a night among the clouds, in whose manifest instability sleet or snow will often be brewing.

THE ICE AXE

Except in the matter of boots, the only technical difference between rock climbs and those involving ice and snow is the use of the ice axe. With this, there are three new danger points: the ice axe's spike, point, and adze.

It soon becomes apparent that this often vital essential is most safely carried horizontally with spike ahead and pick downward, not slung over a shoulder. When the ice axe is used as a cane, the pick ordinarily will be safest forward.

THE CRAMPONS

The ideally hand-forged and tightly fitted crampons, not as indispensable as the axe but also a means of increasing sureness on ice and hard-crusted snow, likewise have points to watch out for. For more stable footing, as well as to prevent blunting or breaking, you'll likely soon get in the habit of removing these climbing irons when more than a short expanse of rock is encountered.

When crampons are packed, corks individually skewered on the tips of the points will guard both their sharpness and everything within reach. Some climbers instead bind their pair of crampons together with the points against a paperback book they've brought for those odd moments.

Any danger of being hung up by a crampon and stumbling, or gouging the opposite shin, can be lessened by tighter or snugged lower clothing, as well as by traveling with your legs farther apart, although not as much as you would when snowshoeing.

THE SAFE GLISSADE

On snow, as occasionally on gravel, glissading may become both an exhilarating and time-saving way to descend, when it can be controlled.

Even when slopes and surfaces are expertly assessed beforehand, there's always the possibility of encountering ice or, during a dry run,

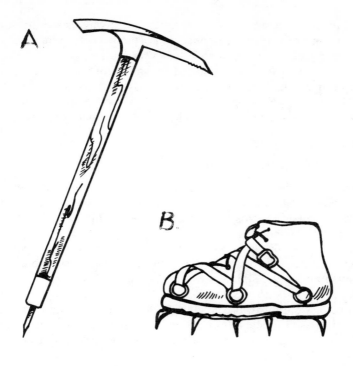
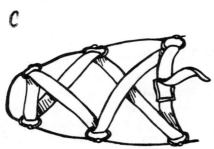

Figure 13. (A) Aside from boots, the difference between rock climbs and those up ice and snow lies in the ice axe. (B) Crampons are hinged, metal frames equipped with sharp spikes, providing stability on ice and hard-crusted snow. (C) Crampons need to be tightly fitted onto the climber's boot. The two must work as a single unit for the stability of the climber.

unmanageable rock and hard clay. Safe exits, away from interruptions like spurs and precipices, can be as important to determine in advance as intended safe finishes.

In glissading, too, the acquired technique of self arrest can mean the difference. That it cannot be depended on solely is emphasized by the fact that on snow slopes, climbing with two companions on a 120-foot rope has proved safer then all three climbing separately.

SWIFTLY CHANGING SURFACES

Snow and ice surfaces can change within minutes, as during the melting balminess of a sudden chinook, then the swift undercutting of these zepher-like breezes by a freezing north wind, with its aftermath of exaggerated slipperiness.

Just the sun can make crust unstable which was firm enough to walk on an hour before, or during some deceptively serene afternoon start slush and stone sliding with increasing devastation.

All this points up the rationale for becoming knowledgeable about the range of weather to be expected in a target area, and thus keeping as far ahead as practical of any related dangers. An alternate route may be the out, or beginning a try for the moonlit top as early as midnight.

Glacial streams, generally more safely forded mornings than afternoons, can be difficult any time the melt is milky, as it becomes when mingling with the finely ground slit frequently eroded from limestone. Then the handle of an ice axe may become the most functional means of determining the obscured bottom ahead.

The often gritty water, incidentally, will be as safe to drink as most in high country.

THE HANSEL-AND-GRETEL RETURN

Getting back gets to be more of a problem in high places where there's snow. Even when strong wind, stung with more of the whiteness, is not rapidly smothering tracks and reducing visibility, fog condensed from vaporizing stretches by the colder air is frequently narrowing an already cloud-shortened day. Ahead is an opaque space where even equilibrium becomes vague.

Any of these conditions can cause disproportionate difficulty on a remote glacier, where retracing your steps may be essential because of crevasses or because there's only a single narrow way off.

A practicable sort of Hansel-and-Gretel precaution is to implant carried uprights, more visible perhaps because of florescent strips fluttering atop, along the outward route about every rope length apart, with concentrations at key points.

THE CONSTANT CREVASSES

The constant portent of crevasses keeps the senses exquisitely tuned during glacier travel, for although awareness and alertness likely will keep you from ever falling into one, the danger remains real enough for precaution. One safeguard sometimes is proceeding at right angles to any open rift, with the realization that others, not all as evident, are apt to parallel it.

A particular peril is fissures hidden beneath snow and ice not stable enough to support your weight. A response to this when companions are along can be traveling roped and well apart, ever moving and always ready for an instant belay.

As with all ice journeying, a slightly lower trough in the surface signals an obvious warning. Transitional areas, as where a snow plane blends into ice, call for special caution, such as testing ahead with ice axe before every step.

Where a snow bridge offers the only route across a crevasse too wide to jump, appraising it from every approachable angle can help establish the reasonableness of any reliance on it. Clues to its stability include thickness, density, and, negatively, surface flaws.

Even when everything says go, you can increase your safety margin when you are with a party by spotting belay points solidly in from the rim before the likeliest member, prodding ahead with axe, cautiously crosses. Then, making as certain as practical that he hasn't moved atop another crevasse, he sets up his own belay point. The others in turn, each probing ahead, follow as nearly as they can in the previous steps—realizing the next may suddenly give away, and that on the return the bridge frozen compactly at sunrise may by afternoon be about to crumble.

GETTING OUT OF CREVASSES

Once in a crevasse, the problem in most cases becomes getting out. A climb sometimes can do it, especially if you're roped to a companion. When you are on your own, it's a matter of whether you are able to manage it before too many limitations are imposed by the usually intense cold. An ice axe, or at least a sturdy knife, can vastly improve either situation.

Any move with a reasonable chance of bettering one's position should be made as soon as possible. Just the donning of additional warm clothing, perhaps carried in a backpack, can extend endurance.

When there's help, tieing a free loop of line around the escape rope and standing with one foot in it sometimes can make a climb feasible. It can then ease an ascent the same way a tree climber's loop does around a trunk, securing each higher position as long as one's weight is on it, and afterward again slipping freely upward to assist the next step.

The others in a party, keeping clear of the edge and of any more rifts, may help by wadding a spare jacket or shirt under the belay rope at the rim, before it adds to the difficulty by cutting into the edge.

Anchoring the belay line to an ice axe may, depending on the situation, free someone to handle a second rope. If this has a noose at the end that the one below can slip under the arms, a steady pull from above can aid the other's progress, which perhaps will be up the first rope hand over hand.

WHEN TWO ARE ALONE TOGETHER

When just you and the one in trouble are alone on a glacier, you can sometimes rappel or climb down if the other is injured. Such a descent will be preferably to one side, where there will be less likelihood of dislodging anything that can complicate the trouble.

Extra clothing, perhaps a chocolate bar, pitons, a spare ice axe, and even some on-the-spot first aid may be enough to get your companion out. At the least it may let you make him or her more comfortable.

You may want to anchor your companion to prevent any further fall while you go for assistance. If so, you'll probably see to it that any constrictive clothing and equipment is loosened enough to enable freer breathing and circulation. Such articles as crampons you may help detach to eliminate even the chance of unnecessary chilling.

Then after all possible assurance, you likely will get back up, mark the spot as obviously as expedient with helicopter rescue also in mind, make as sure as you can by landmarks and any other means that you'll be able to pinpoint the place quickly, and start for help.

Chapter 16

The Mountain World

The proportion of oxygen in the air is almost the same at sea level as atop the highest mountain. What differs is density and pressure.

It's the compression of the surrounding atmosphere, lowering gradually as it does with highering altitude, that forces this life-maintaining element into the bloodstream. Although the oxygen saturation of the arterial blood has dropped only some 3 percent at five thousand feet, it's fallen more than 20 percent at fifteen thousand feet.

HYPOXIA, ITS CARE AND FEEDING

As air pressure decreases the higher you climb, the greater becomes the possibility of hypoxia. This is brought about by inadequate oxygen, thereby suggesting its own cure. Showing up in the occasional individual at as low as six thousand feet, hypoxia's symptoms include headache, vague uneasiness, exhaustion, nausea, vomiting, weakliness, shortness of breath, and insomnia. These indications are usually worse the next morning, then slowly improve.

Below eight thousand feet, however, such troubles from this cause are rare. Some experience them between eight thousand and ten thousand feet. Above fourteen thousand feet most lowlanders become involved. Overall, the young are most frequently bothered.

Two of hypoxia's symptoms themselves generally right matters. Accelerating heartbeat and quickening respiration usually combine to readjust the oxygen flow to the tissues effectively. Hyperventilation, in fact, becomes necessary in the higher altitudes when maximal arterial oxygen content is to be maintained. Even someone previously acclimatized who journeys back down to sea level may be susceptible for several days after returning.

Any tendency toward dehydration can be easily offset by eating clean snow or ice along the way or, if you prefer, by stopping to melt and drink it. Aspirin and the like generally make such symptoms as headache more tolerable. Pure oxygen, when a supply is carried, can right matters with dramatic swiftness.

ACUTE MOUNTAIN SICKNESS

Although acute mountain sickness alone does not dictate descent, a lower altitude is indicated for progressive, more severe cases. Generally, a temporary halt will be enough, especially if any further climbing is slower. When a long sought peak is just ahead, above which there's only the wind, you'll likely be revived by brief rest, deep breathing, and a few bites of some quickly assimilated food such as chocolate.

Rapidity of ascent is the most significant factor common to acute mountain sickness. Those who fly from lowland homes to high country, and immediately start climbing, are especially susceptible.

But prior high altitude living brings no immunity to acute mountain sickness. Neither does physical conditioning. However, the longer you spend adapting to the new altitudes, the less will be the likelihood of difficulty.

RETINAL HEMORRHAGE

Some degree of retinal hemorrhage is a common response to high altitude. It shows up among a quarter to a fifth of those climbing above fourteen thousand feet. It is not usually noticed unless the part of the eye opposite the pupil is examined. When you do become aware of any disorder, this is generally because of floating specks, dark spots, or blurring vision.

Extreme physical exertion seems to increase incidence, the trouble often progressing as you climb higher. Treatment, again, is descent.

Although the odd black spot occasionally stays, the majority of retinal hemorrhages right themselves spontaneously with the eyesight remaining as keen as ever.

THOSE SUDDEN DRY COUGHS

A climber's sudden dry coughing with no apparent cause may be the beginning of high altitude pulmonary edema, no longer rare these days when even commercial airlines are booking flights to once remote mountain vastnesses. Early recognition and prompt descent remain the two major routes to recovery.

This fluid accumulation in the lungs generally starts twenty-four to seventy-two hours after such high altitudes are reached. Its incidence is disproportionately greater among enthusiasts not yet twenty-one years old who speedily ascend to lofty regions.

Often it appears at night when, despite inactivity, the telltale signs of labored breathing, aching chest, and relentless coughing become evident. Such previously considered symptoms of acute mountain sickness as headache, sleeplessness, dizziness, nausea, and racing heartbeat can accompany these indications in varying degrees.

With individuals who venture into tall country characteristically absorbing discomfort with no outward or usually even inner complaint, the initial difficulties many times are not readily detected. As they progress, however, shallow and rapid breathing can take on a telltale irregular, gurgling undertone.

There's also the likelihood of decreasing blood pressure and increasing temperature. Mucus that's coughed up sometimes begins showing froth and blood.

Without treatment, the condition tends to become increasingly severe with alarming speed. Getting back down below eight thousand feet usually leads to the gradual disappearance of the symptoms within one to three days.

The basic precaution continues to be leisurely ascent. Ascending some 1,000 feet a day to a height of 14,000 feet, then about 500 feet daily above this level ordinarily works. On such a city-surrounded American peak as 14,410-foot Mount Rainier where such guidelines are customarily disregarded, most climbers through its four life zones stay at high altitudes only briefly, not long enough usually to trigger the trouble.

BETTER DOWN THAN DEAD

Cerebral edema is a severe form of altitude sickness, occurring typically above twelve thousand feet, from which descent becomes unusually urgent. The disability not only carries high risk of permanent damage if the time from unconsciousness to reaching a lower level is prolonged, but without one's going down, death becomes almost inevitable.

Like other oxygen-related high-country illnesses, cerebral edema is most likely to appear after rapid ascent. Its onset usually begins two to three days after arrival in the rarefied atmosphere, with increasingly severe headache and dizziness usually with vomiting. Convulsions may follow.

Unless lower altitudes are soon reached the disease almost always advances from lethargy, to stupor, coma, and death. Cerebral edema, fortunately, continues to be rare.

WHEN A CLIMBER STOPS BREATHING

The occasional climber, beset by oxygen insufficiency, loses consciousness and even stops breathing. Then staying alive can hinge on immediate mouth-to-mouth respiration. If the individual is still not breathing well after being given oxygen or moved below ten thousand feet, such artificial respiration should be continued.

At any altitude when undue breathing difficulty continues despite the entry of pure oxygen through a tightly applied mask, artificial respiration should be started with minimum delay, preferably by the back-pressure-and-arm-lift method.

The mouth-to-mouth procedure detailed in relation to swimming will also work in the mountains wherever there's sufficient oxygen pressure in the air. But when oxygen is being supplied by tank and mask, life can depend on instituting different measures in a hurry.

Then when a companion stops breathing, stretch him face down. Bend his elbows, placing one hand on the other to pillow his head. (See Fig. 14A.) Remove the mask long enough to make sure his mouth is clear, at the same time pulling his tongue forward. Once the mask is back in place keep watching for vomiting, ready to clear it when necessary.

Kneel beside his head. If it's more comfortable, straddle the head with both knees. (See Fig. 14B.) Otherwise, set your free foot near an elbow.

Either way you'll then be in position to place both hands on the flat of his back, the bases of the thumbs just below a line between the

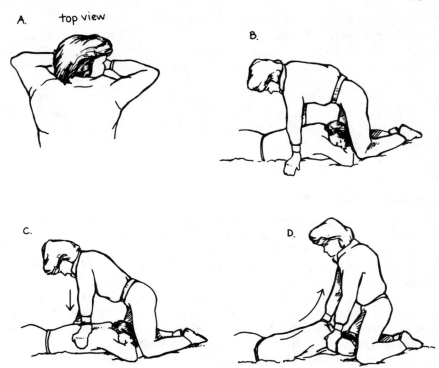

Figure 14. When a mountain-climbing companion ceases to breathe, this resuscitation method is appropriate (used in conjunction with an oxygen mask, not shown; see text for a-d).

armpits. With the tips of your thumbs touching, spread your fingers downward and outward. Rock forward until your arms are approximately vertical, allowing the weight of your upper body to press downward slowly and steadily. (See Fig. 14C.)

Without adding an extra push, lift your hands. Start to rock slowly backward, at the same time grasping his arms just above the elbows. Keeping your own arms straight, draw his upward and toward you. Let this happen naturally as you move back, with just enough lift to feel tension and resistance at his shoulders. (See Fig. 14D.)

This arm lift pulls on his upper muscles, arches his back, and relieves the pressure on his chest. The action triggers the suction of air into his lungs. Replacing, not dropping, his arms on the ground completes the cycle.

Important, as with all such lifegiving procedures, is establishing and maintaining rhythm. The sequence in this instance is: press, release, lift, release. The release periods should be as brief as you can make them. The cycle should be repeated about ten to twelve times a minute.

Success may mean continuing more than two hours. Settling into the rocking motion makes this easier, particularly as positions and even participants can be changed without adverse effects as long as the rhythm is maintained unbroken.

IF AN ARM IS FRACTURED

If the companion in trouble also has a seriously injured arm, try another pressure method of artificial resuscitation.

Once he is prone with the sound arm bent, turn his head to the side where it will be supported by that hand. The other hand may be above his head. (See Fig. 15A.)

Straddle him at the hips, either knee on the ground and your free foot directly opposite it. Fingers spread and pointing outward, your hands go just below his shoulder blades so that your nearly meeting thumbs are an inch or two from his spine. (See Fig. 15B.)

Then when you lean forward with elbows straight, the weight of your upper body can press almost directly downward, slowly and steadily forcing air out of his lungs. (See Fig. 15C.)

Release the pressure by taking away your hands, abruptly and without any last-instance shove. Rocking backward at the same time, grasp his hips several inches below his waist, just slipping your fingers under his hip bones where they touch the ground.

Lift both hips, bringing them upward some four to six inches and toward you. This way his abdomen will sag downward, his diaphragm descend, and air will be sucked into his lungs. Keeping your elbows straight will concentrate the effort in your shoulders and back, rather than in your otherwise more quickly tiring arms. (See Fig. 15D.)

Replace the victim's hips in their original position, never letting them just fall. This will complete the cycle: press, release, lift, release. It's then a matter of settling into repeating this sequence, uniformly and steadily, about ten to twelve times a minute. Again, each release period should be as brief as possible.

Continuing the rhythm is the important factor whenever there's a change of position or participant. When just shifting your knees, you'll probably find this easiest immediately after a press-release phase. When

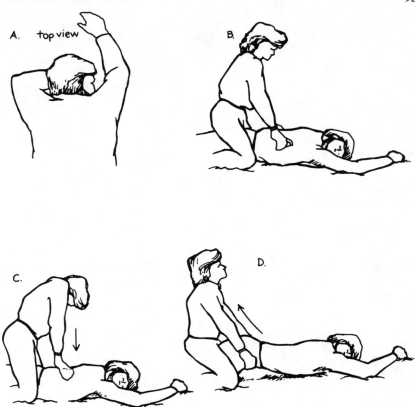

Figure 15. If the companion in trouble also has a badly injured arm, this method of artificial respiration may be the one that will keep him alive. (See text for a–d.)

there's a relief, generally the second person can take over most conveniently from the side opposite the knee you have on the ground, in time to begin the next press-release phase.

When you're alone and have to wait for your strength to catch up, the safest way is to continue just the press-release at the slightly faster speed of twelve to fifteen times a minute. Then as soon as you reasonably can, resume the full cycle. Or fit in the hip-lift every second, third, or fourth time, or as often as you can manage.

Once natural breathing starts, the ideal follow-up is the same as with other methods of artificial respiration, within any bounds imposed by the particular situation.

III

SUMMER

I walked with a companion for twelve miles through a beautiful forest, from one camp to another. It was the month of April and nature was at her best. Trees, shrubs, and creepers were in full bloom. Gaily colored butterflies flitted from flower to flower, and the air, filled with the scent of flowers, throbbed with the song of birds. At the end of the day my companion was asked if he had enjoyed the walk, and he answered, "No. The road was very rough."

Jim Corbett

Chapter 17

Swimming Well Can Get You in Trouble

Not always realized is how much more staying safe in and on the water involves than just being able to swim well. By overestimating this ability, the expert swimmer is often the one who drowns in an emergency, as by striking for shore from a capsized canoe despite unrealized odds, while the duffer who prudently, if necessarily, stays with the craft and strokes landward is the one who makes it.

Drowning's principal causes include the failure to recognize unduly dangerous conditions, ineptness in getting out of trouble once it does develop, ignorance about how to help someone in distress with optimum safety for both, and panic, which is a factor in most swimming mishaps.

The counteroffensive to have ready, before such irrational fear has a chance to overwhelm judgment, begins with understanding what is actually involved. When you know that, proficiency, confidence, and dependable initiative follow naturally. Then when there is difficulty, your conditioned reaction will be positive and concentrated on eliminating the actual danger. Disregarded, panic itself often creates the danger.

ADAPTING TO HAZARDOUS CURRENTS

Staying safe in a dangerous current ordinarily lies in not battling it head on, unless for a short distance when there is no better choice. It is best to swim with and, when the situation calls for it, across such movement. This generally means coming ashore some distance from the landing intended, but it also usually means getting there unscathed.

The majority of the river and ocean currents that can get you in trouble follow the shoreline. When a tidal tow which runs out from the coast is unexpectedly encountered, escape frequently depends on easing along with it until out of its influence, only then striking for the beach.

The boiling water beneath falls, as well as in other spots where rivers deepen, sometimes traps a swimmer by drawing him or her down, again and again, in its whirling undertow. Here, as when you're being swept toward a rock after a boating miscalculation, evasion lies in disregarding instinct and diving.

The strongest flows, sweeping the bottom, then can shoot you safely into the clear.

THE STRANGLEHOLD DILEMMA

Terror, fatigue, and in the most desperate circumstances the instinct to keep breathing, often cause someone in trouble in the water to grab at the nearest likely support. Despite all precautions, one day this last-chance support may be you.

If the individual in distress is a swimmer you're approaching in a rescue attempt, you can at least be ready for any necessary evasion. It's a lot more frightening when suddenly you are among several others overboard in a boating accident, and one of them clutches you around the neck from behind with a stranglehold, too unexpectedly for you even to clamp your chin down and around to protect your windpipe. Before the grip tightens, though, you'll likely have time for a quick breath.

Continuing to get air will also be the other person's overwhelming concern, which means his every urge will be to keep his own head above water. Your best response usually will be to deliberately sink, drawing the victim down with you. Once he is underwater, his instinct will change to getting away from you in his franticness to regain the surface.

Coolness and the ability to handle yourself in the water generally mean staying safe in such situations. Familiarity with ways of breaking the different holds can add even more of an edge.

Figure 16. This rescuer gives the victim a sense of assurance by supporting her so she can breathe freely, while at the same time he stays out of the clutching zone in case she suddenly panics.

OVERBOARD FULLY CLOTHED

Unexpectedly going overboard fully clothed results in a significant number of drownings, both by constricting movement and by increasing weight. Unless there's not enough time or unless the distance is too short to matter, escaping on your own commonly involves treading water long enough to disrobe.

Sometimes removing your footwear is enough—taking a deep breath, bending forward in a float, and using both hands on each shoe in turn, lifting your head whenever more air is required.

In any event, the least tiring way to swim while clothed is with a stroke that lets you keep your arms and legs underwater. Anything else usually means fighting the growing restraint and burden of waterlogging garments whenever a limb is brought above the surface. Such squandered energy can make the difference.

There are times when garb can help, however, as during prolonged exposure where there's support and in really cold water. Warm woolens are even advisable for canoeists not wearing wet suits, on the frigid lakes and rivers of this continent's back country.

EXTENDING SWIMMING ENJOYMENT

Such unreliable supports as beach balls and inflated inner tubes too frequently give beginners enough misplaced assurance to venture farther than they can handle themselves. Too often these supports then get or give away. Especially in the unconfined open while learning to swim, it's reasonable to keep to shallows no deeper than the neck and where, ideally, the shore slopes away gradually.

Swimming waters will continue to be safest when selected in relation to both situation and ability. Swimming with someone else can extend both enjoyment and boundaries, especially when the companion is competent to see to your well-being, too, should ever the need arise.

There are always the hazards to remain alert for: outriders from civilization like jagged metal and broken glass, slippery and unstable approaches, underwater obstructions like submerged boulders and sunken logs, holes and other unexpected drop-offs, vegetation that can become entangling, sly currents, occasional quicksand, erratic surf, rocks and reefs that can tear the skin, and sometimes aquatic life such as jellyfish which are injurious to touch.

SWIMMING ENDURANCE AND STRENGTH

You need, if you're the average active swimmer, to eat some sixteen hundred to two thousand calories to keep going with full efficiency. Despite the fads and abuses, the principles of weight loss and gain in most cases remain simple. To lose a pound of fat, you must work off about thirty-five hundred calories more than you eat.

Conversely, gaining a pound of lean muscle means exercising vigorously and eating about twenty-five hundred calories more than what's basically required. No amount of megavitamins, liquid proteins, or the controversial anabolic steroids whose safety is questionable, seems to alter these underlying facts.

But for particular individuals in particular situations the physiologically sound high-performance diets, including the glycogen-loading and glycogen-depleting techniques, may enhance energy when endurance will be a factor, as when making a long-distance swim.

BASICS OF RESCUE

Offshore emergencies vary, but ordinarily not even a trained and experienced lifeguard should attempt a direct swimming rescue if there's a way to avoid it by boat, surfboard, or other means. Even when an in-water approach becomes necessary, the expert usually prefers to extend a belt, towel, roped life preserver, or such while remaining beyond the victim's grasp.

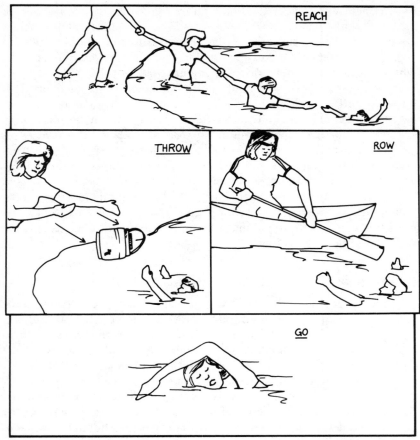

Figure 17. Not even an experienced lifeguard should attempt a direct swimming rescue if it can be avoided by one of these four options.

Easy to disregard in the surge of impulse and emotion immediate with such a crisis is the answer to a single hard question: How can it help for two to drown instead of one?

REALITIES OF IMMERSION CHILL

.   Until you've plunged into a mountain stream, it's difficult to realize how numbing many of this continent's likeliest boating, fishing, and other vacation waters remain in midsummmer, and how quickly even someone swimming in them by choice can lose all ability to function.

A personal flotation device that will float you at the start can be expected to support you indefinitely. Cold, however, can still do you in within minutes.

The common killer is subnormal body warmth, immersion hypothermia brought about by the loss of inner body heat to the water. Once human temperature is dampened into the 85°F. range, which is regarded as the point where death begins, even someone in top physical condition risks cardiac arrest.

In water warmer than 70°F., where natural heat production can keep pace with heat loss, fatigue leading to ultimate exhaustion becomes the limiting factor. But exhaustion if not unconsciousness can be expected within as little as fifteen minutes in lakes and rivers just above freezing, and demise inside fifteen to forty-five minutes.

Warm woolens and the special wet suits, as well as the protective insulation judiciously added to buoyancy jackets by such North American concerns as the Stearne Manufacturing Company, so extend all these cold-water limits that the alert canoeist or other boater, keeping reasonably close to where he or she can get ashore in the unlikelihood of an emergency, is far safer on remote lakes and rivers than in freeway traffic.

TO SWIM OR NOT

Even when the cause of death in cold water is recorded as drowning, what often comes first is unconsciousness brought about by one's midbody temperature falling beneath the constant level necessary for the heart and brain and other vital organs to continue proper functioning.

This heat loss can be hastened by swimming. Then as much as half of the body's insulating mechanism may shut off, partly by the shunting of warm blood to the arms and legs, and partly because stirring the surrounding water makes it absorb body heat quicker.

Small individuals cool faster than large, thin quicker than fat. The average woman can be caught in the middle. Although she has more subcutaneous body fat insulation than the average man, she is also smaller.

If shore is within reach, get there as quickly as you reasonably can. When this involves drifting with a capsized craft, the more of your body you get out of the cold water the better. Cold water can pull heat from the body over twenty-five times faster than air of the same temperature.

To conserve your warmth in either circumstance, gather yourself tightly together in the fetal or self-huddle position.

SOME STEPS TO RECOVERY

Recovery from immersion hypothermia depends on rewarming the body's core temperature while keeping the reviving circulation from speeding cold surface blood back into the midbody so fast it cools it further.

A first step is to get the individual out of the wind and wet. Next, remove all soaked clothing, which can cause significantly greater heat loss than relatively still air. If no better way is available to get the other warm, use body-to-body contact under whatever covers may be at hand, such as inside a sleeping bag.

Keep the victim as still and quiet as possible, throughout. If there's difficulty breathing, keep the air passage open. If respiration continues deteriorating or stops, start mouth-to-mouth resuscitation.

Chapter 18

Women and the Water

Feminine and masculine physiological mechanisms are much the same. Both women and men reach their overall sports prime usually between the ages of twenty-two and thirty.

Swimming is an exception. Girls often reach their peaks when fifteen or sixteen years old. Important to feminine swimmers, too, is that generally even the slimmer have proportionately 10 percent to 20 percent more fat than men, with the added buoyancy and the better resistance to cold this gives.

The feminine sector continues to engage in more and more outdoor recreation that until very recently was considered almost exclusively male. Women are participating more vigorously, too, in the traditional sports which always included them.

The medical profession is seeing a great many injuries once familiar only to those treating ballet dancers, circus performers, rodeo riders, and the then rare professional women athletes. With all this has come a new awareness about women and recreation.

THE FACTS OF FLUID RETENTION

"The old wives' dictum that menstruating women should not participate in athletics finds few advocates today,'' observes Dr. James A. Nicholas, probably the country's most prominent expert on athletic capabilities. ''In most cases, there is no reason for restrictions on a woman's activity. But there are a few provisions to keep in mind.''

Premenstrual fluid retention, he points out, can be marked enough in some individuals to hamper their movement, with feet and ankles swelling and slowing them down, particularly in warm weather. At the same time, this condition makes them more susceptible to accidents.

Even with a strained ankle, healing will be slower than it would be if the swelling wasn't there to complicate matters. In such cases both the strain and the edema can be troublesome for months.

Girls are most vulnerable to injuries at the beginning of menstruation, with their injury rate multiplying during the span of rapid growth accompanying this initiation to womanhood. Doctor Nicholas finds girls who reach this beginning at the same age are more similar to each other in terms of development than to those sharing the same birth date but starting menstruation at a different time.

PREGNANCY'S PREFERRED RECREATION

During pregnancy, most outdoor recreation can be safely and even advantageously continued. After the fifth month, however, studies indicate the advisability of a sojourn from the contact sports and such others as skiing.

Weight and fluid retention are usually setting up problems by about the seventh month. When this is accompanied by swelling at the joints, excess stress at these parts can be damaging.

Swimming then becomes the preferred choice, now that it's well to curb exhausting physical activity. Even in late pregnancy swimming is generally recommended as a suitable sport, the water buoyantly easing any muscular strain. At the same time it can be comfortably cooling the body.

SHAPING UP FOR BATHING SUITS

Too many women and girls fear that strengthening exercises will cause them to build masculine bulk, but normal hormone levels naturally prevent this.

The feminine fashion has long been stretching to loosen muscles and develop tone. The trouble is, most girls and women incline to be loose-jointed. The answer for them is to make their muscles not more elastic but stronger.

This can be done by using weights—the reason these days why just about all big-time professional male athletes are noticeably brawnier, especially around their necks which often start at the ears and work out to the shoulders.

"The old tales about weight lifting making you muscle-bound were terribly exaggerated," says Clyde Emrich who's long directed weight training for the National Football League's Chicago Bears. He points out that the impetus for the widespread acceptance of weights started about twenty years ago when scientists, with the help of stop-action films, began examining in earnest the intricacies of sports physiology.

"You start with the athlete's body type and the sport, and you use common sense. The big, bunchy muscles you see among the so-called bodybuilders will limit flexibility. What I emphasize is lifts involving the full extension of the limbs. If you take the weights all the way up and down, your freedom of movement won't be diminished," he advises.

"And even with things that don't take much strength, a strong muscle is easier to control than a weak one."

WOMEN AND SWIMMER'S SHOULDER

Swimmer's shoulder, usually linked under another name with injuries to baseball pitchers, afflicts women as well as men. Even middle-aged women who don't keep in condition sometimes court such ruptures with just abrupt everyday exertions.

Because females have only about half as much muscle mass as males in the shoulder joints and soft tissue construction, this mechanically complex area of union can be exceptionally vulnerable. An answer lies in developing these muscles along with those in the adjoining spinal system, thus strengthening and streamlining the entire trunk.

One way to begin, suggests Meredith Melvin and Dr. James A. Nicholas in *The Female Patient,* is to sit with your upper back and shoulders pressed against a straight-backed chair. These medical authorities say the best weight to start with is the heaviest one you can hold in your fingertips while performing the following exercise painlessly a dozen times with a steady arm.

Hold the weight in front of your shoulder, hand outward and elbow level out to the side. Press it straight ahead as far as you can reach. Then move it slowly and flatly sideways, still at arm's length. When you feel a strain in the front of the shoulder, bring the weight gradually back across the body until the tugging sensation moves to

Figure 18. To develop muscles in the shoulders and adjoining spinal system, sit with your upper back and shoulders pressed against a straight-backed chair, performing this exercise with the heaviest weight you can hold in your fingertips.

that shoulder's back. Then slowly return the weight straight ahead, and next to where it started. Repeat with the other arm. As your strength increases with daily repetitions, it can be beneficial to add more presses and weight.

Chapter 19

Why Drown? Why Choke?

Anyone not getting oxygen cannot live long, so being ready for any breathing difficulty can make the difference. Preparedness ordinarily involves not only learning the most effective emergency procedures, but practicing all the stages (except for forceful thrusts) of artificial respiration, at least up to mouth-to-mouth breathing. Even this phase can be made familiar with the help of a portable device consisting of a short tube with a mask at one end to cover a victim's face for maximum efficiency.

More and more, there is less and less reason for anyone to drown or otherwise suffocate.

THE HEIMLICH MANEUVER

"The first step on the treatment of drowning should be the Heimlich Maneuver in the supine position—patient lying on back, face forward—in order to get the water out of the airway and lungs," advised Henry J. Heimlich, M.D., professor of advance clinical sciences at Xavier University. Dr. Heimlich is the developer of the new technique credited already with saving numerous lives of people who are choking on such things as food.

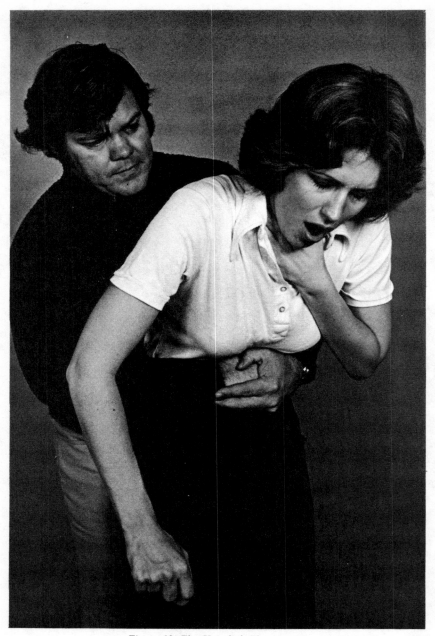

Figure 19. The Heimlich Maneuver

"In this instance," in connection with drowning, Dr. Heimlich told me, "the victim's head should be turned to the side to allow water to flow out of the mouth (as differentiated from performing the Heimlich Maneuver for choking victims, when turning the head to the side twists the throat and does not allow a solid object to be expelled). Repeat the Heimlich Maneuver until no water flows from the mouth. Wipe this out and, if the patient is not breathing, proceed with mouth to mouth."

To perform these preliminaries, you should straddle the drowning victim, one knee either side of his lower hips. Put your fist, held by your second hand, thumbside against the other's abdomen just below the rib cage and slightly above the navel. Then repeatedly apply hard, rapid, upward thrusts.

OR NO THRUSTS

Do not use abdominal thrusts for a drowning victim because of the danger of driving water or other material from the stomach into the air passages where aspiration could move it into the lungs, states the American Red Cross, adding that it is not possible to pour water out of the lungs, and no attempt should be made to do so.

If there is any obstruction in the airway, the Red Cross recommends more force in blowing into the individual's mouth or nose than in other respiratory emergencies, to drive air through any blocking water.

WHICHEVER

In any event the rescuer's beginning mouth-to-mouth respiration while still in the water, clinging perhaps to a bouyant bedroll, is not too soon. However, it is better to avoid any unnecessary delay in reaching shore or other sanctuary.

A NEW WAY TO SAVE LIFE

Anywhere or at any time, anyone choking, perhaps on food, may be unable to get his breath, inhale, or even speak. If he's standing or sitting when such total obstruction occurs, the Heimlich Maneuver can be started by getting behind him and putting both of your arms around his waist. With your elbows winged out, apply hard, quick, upward thrusts.

A number of physicians now say the long-recommended slaps on the back can make matters worse. A particular hazard with children, they believe, is that the foreign object may thus be forced against the underside of the young person's larynx where it may become trapped. This can be even more likely, it's said, if the child is held upside down when slapped, as many manuals still advise.

With the Heimlich Maneuver, you exert force to press the diaphragm upward, compressing the air in the lungs and directly expelling

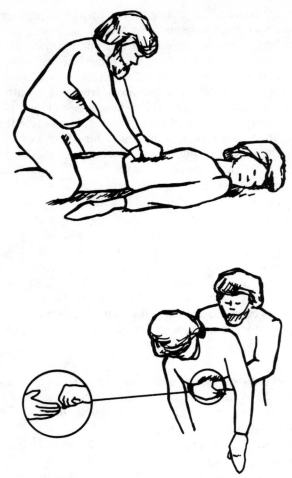

Figure 20. The Heimlich Maneuver

whatever's blocking the breathing passage. Without this being opened, death by strangulation is certain.

The maneuver can cause injury. However, the individual will survive only if he or she becomes able to breathe again within four minutes.

THE REVISED RED CROSS ROUTINE

Acknowledging the contribution made by Henry J. Heimlich, M.D., for the development of his new maneuver, the American Red Cross and others now recognize the importance of the abdominal thrusts—

sometimes called the Heimlich Maneuver—in saving the lives of choking victims.

The long familiar back blows, which Dr. Heimlich asserts may further impact an object stuck in the airway as well as waste time better used thrusting, are still continued in the Red Cross's revised sequence. They suggest backslaps sharply struck four times in rapid succession centrally between the shoulder blades with the heel of the hand. These are quickly followed by four thrusts, all repeated if necessary.

Suspending an infant or child by the heels, with which Professor Heimlich also took issue, has been revised in recent material. The newer American Red Cross advice is that the conscious victim should be supported face up, as on an adult's thigh, with his or her head lowered.

Press four times with your fingertips between the nipples, up and down the sternum rather than across it. These chest thrusts are similar to those for an adult except they are one-handed and reasonably lighter. Four sharp heel-of-hand back blows, followed by four chest thrusts, are now recommended, repeated rapidly until the foreign matter is expelled.

MOUTH-TO-MOUTH

On-the-spot action quickly determines life or death when breathing stops not only as a result of drowning, but also as a result of smoke inhalation during a forest fire, electric shock in the course of a lightning storm, cardiac arrest, or even an insect bite.

Most important is starting at once. Next is being sure the victim's air passage is open.

During unconsciousness the airway usually is obstructed to some degree. The first of the three major causes is liquid, false teeth, or other alien matter in the mouth or throat. What can't be picked out is usually cleared by wiping it away or sweeping it out with the index and middle fingers.

The second common obstruction occurs when the relaxed jaw allows the tongue, which is attached, to fall back and block the throat. A forefinger can hook it free.

A third possible hindrance is the position of the neck. When this is bent forward with the chin close to the chest, there is a tendency for the throat to become kinked. The airway can be opened and kept open by bending the head as far back as reasonable so that the front of the neck is stretched, at the same time holding the lower jaw forward in a sword-swallowing position.

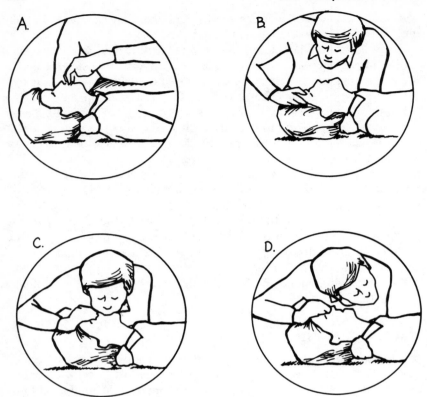

Figure 21. Mouth-to-mouth resuscitation: (A) Check with your finger to make sure nothing is obscuring victim's air passage. (B) Tilt victim's head back and lift neck to open air passage. (C) Holding victim's nostrils closed, cover his mouth with your own and exhale. (D) Lift your head so that he can exhale naturally and listen for the air leaving his mouth.

ARTIFICIAL RESPIRATION WHEN YOU'RE RIGHT-HANDED

If you are right-handed, it will be easier to approach the victim's head from his left side, as he lies on his back.

Press your left thumb between his front teeth, and then pull his lower jaw forcefully outward until his lower teeth are farther forward than the upper. As long as he is unconscious, hold his jaw in this position with your thumb. If there's concern about being bitten, protect your finger with a handkerchief or similar wrapping.

Squeeze the victim's nostrils together between the forefinger and thumb of your right hand. Then inhale deeply, cover his mouth tightly with yours, and exhale vigorously and rapidly. Block any air leakage from the victim's nose by pressing his nasal openings shut with your cheek. With a small child, press your mouth over both its nose and mouth while breathing out, this time more gently.

The victim's chest should rise. If it doesn't, immediately recheck the position of his chin and head. See if the tongue somehow may be obstructing his air passage. After any necessary adjustments, try again, if necessary blowing more forcefully.

Each time the victim's chest rises, lift your mouth so he can exhale naturally. With an adult, blow one vigorous breath twelve times a minute. With a small child, your exhalations should be shallower and twenty times a minute. Rather than becoming concerned with split-second timing, concentrate on settling smoothly into a steady rhythm.

Improving skin color can indicate the procedure is working. So can a readily discernible pulse beat when there didn't seem to be one before and the pupils of the eyes beginning to get smaller.

With cold water accidents in particular, the thread of life is often extraordinarily prolonged. Success comes sometimes after two hours of artificial respiration, in relays when assistance is at hand. Even when there are no signs of life, if the victim has been underwater less than an hour there is hope.

You'll already if possible have sent for outside help. However, properly performed artificial respiration can be as effective as a mechanical resuscitator with an output of pure oxygen. It's because we normally exhale three-fourths of the oxygen we breathe that all this works.

TIGHT JAWS AND INFANTS

With the usual child under the age of three, the above procedure is not practical because your thumb interferes with mouth-to-mouth contact. There is difficulty, too, with someone of any age whose mouth cannot be adequately opened.

As always, there are ways around the problems. The initial preparations are the same. Instead of putting your thumb in the victim's mouth, however, grasp both sides of the infant's lower jaw just beneath his ear lobes. Lift the jaw forcefully outward until his bottom teeth are ahead of his upper ones. Then shove the under lip down with both thumbs, while continuing to hold the lower jaw forward as long as he remains unconscious.

Figure 22. Mouth-to-mouth resuscitation with a child.

Again, inhale deeply and cover the infant's mouth tightly with yours. Place your mouth over both his mouth and nose.

The remainder of the pattern remains unchanged.

WATER IN THE STOMACH

The drowning victim often swallows considerable water. When you exhale those first few breaths into his airway, this water may be pushed into his throat by the pressure exerted through the diaphragm by his expanding lungs.

Keeping alert for the possible results, all you have to do at the decisive moment is roll his head to the handier side so that fluid and anything else can drain. The upper abdomen can be compressed to help things along. Or the individual can be rolled over and lifted with your hands under his stomach.

Then, after clearing his mouth as far back as may be necessary, resume the rhythm of exhaled-air respiration.

AIR IN THE STOMACH

Although stomach inflation rarely occurs when the correct technique is followed, it does happen when the airway is restricted, as by inadequate support of head and lower jaw, or when the blowing is overenergetic.

A tip-off is when the victim's abdomen starts bulging. Although such distending is not dangerous, inflation of the lungs is easier when the stomach is empty.

The solution again is simple. Just interrupt blowing in breaths long enough to press the victim's upper abdomen with your free hand. Since this burping may also bring about vomiting, be ready to roll his head to the preferable side and to clear his mouth afterward, and then hasten back into the beat, probably this time more effectively.

AFTER AND BEFORE

Unless assistance has made it practical sooner, when an individual starts breathing see that his clothing is loosened or, if wet, removed. Then when possible treat for shock by lowering his head and shoulders, elevating his legs, and reassuring him with as much comfortable warmth as can be managed.

Such positive dealing with this additional and too often fatal potential has a greater chance of being effective when it is instituted before the victim has a chance actually to lapse into shock.

You won't want to interrupt rhythmical artifical respiration unnecessarily, of course, before he does begin breathing.

THE THROWBACK WHICH SAVES LIVES

Lives of victims, especially those submerged in cold water, sometimes are saved as the result of the atavistic Nemiroff Syndrome.

"Near-drowning victims have better survivability than we would normally expect, especially after submersion in cold water," Dr. Martin J. Nemiroff finds. "Hypothermia is often present and is another protective mechanism, as reduced oxygen requirements result. Therefore, aggressive resuscitation, especially as the patient is actively rewarmed, is often successful."

The University of Michigan researcher says the reason is coldness which alerts the response called the mammalian diving reflex. At the same time it lowers the body's need for oxygen. As a result, the breathing stops while the blood flow to the skin, muscle, and other tissues not necessarily affected by low oxygen levels shuts off. The blood flows instead to the highly vulnerable heart, lungs, and brain.

Somebody who has been under water colder than 70°F. for up to thirty minutes, and sometimes longer, has "an excellent chance for survival and complete recovery with very aggressive, immediate resuscitation and rescue breathing—pressing rhythmically on the breast-bone, at the same time or intermittently breathing air into the mouth."

Complete mental and physical recovery is especially characteristic of individuals not yet out of their teens.

Doctor Nemiroff's evidence indicates that all human beings have this mammalian diving reflex very shortly after birth. As they grow older, it becomes less potent.

Chapter 20

The Satisfaction in Stay-Safe Sailing

Basic sailboat safety, like that of other watercraft, lies largely in balance. Landlubbers discover this with that first step aboard the smaller and lighter wind-driven classes. The nearer to the edge that step is, the greater the tendency to tip.

As for striding on forward, this often means teetering on a submerged bow. Even the greenest beginner learns early to place that lead leg close to the centerline, at or near the sailboat's widest part.

Once in the handling and sailing area, you feel your heft steadying the craft, signifying to the dewiest tyro that whenever anyone moves out of the cockpit, weight apportionment and its consequences can quickly again be a problem.

A practical way to start savoring the satisfaction that lies in understanding sailboat balance, a lot of us find, is by experimenting with the craft in shallow water and by taking the time to study its responses at moorage.

The principle cause of sailboat accidents is overloading. Because the sensitive relationship between weight and balance is so critical, common sense lies in never taking aboard too many or too much, particularly when there can be more lasting enjoyment in a second trip.

GETTING BACK UNDER WAY

That small sailboats sometimes capsize is no surprise to even the most land-bound. Not so generally realized, especially when a newcomer first goes over, is the urgency for making sure no one is trapped beneath the sails.

Then, with everyone perhaps clinging safely to the craft, will ordinarily be soon enough to take into account location and drift. Also, when it may help matters, you can let loose the anchor if that is practical.

Righting the boat may involve loosening the sails beforehand, especially those made with one of the more traditional fabrics such as the quickly saturated cottons. Newer materials are more often nonabsorbent, whereupon the only immediate obstacle may be wind instead of weight.

Any centerboard should be down far enough to give you leverage, although leeboards may have to be shifted out of the way. Then everybody can grasp the exposed gunwale, brace their feet on or against any centerboard, and mass all available heaviness into bringing the sailer upright.

Aboard once more, you can look to rigging and rudder, attend to bailing, check that anchor, and see about getting back under way.

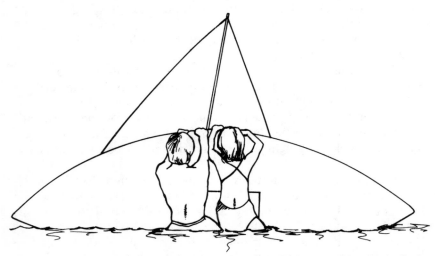

Figure 23. To right a sailboat, passengers should grasp the exposed gunwale, brace their feet on or against the centerboard, and use their combined weight to bring the sailboat upright.

RIGHTS-OF-WAY

Although the sailing craft generally has the right-of-way over a powerboat, you'll probably accept this as a point seldom prudent to argue, in view of the odds in the event of impact. Too, a larger and less maneuverable powerboat does have the right-of-way over a small sailboat.

All such rules of the road are superseded when following any would make danger of collision or in navigation immediate. Then it's each handler's responsibility to do his or her best to avoid any trouble.

LETTING GO THE HOOK

When you're just getting your sea legs, usually you won't drop the hook in water deeper than twenty-five feet. For this, at least one anchor and two hundred feet of line may well be stowed aboard. To allow for emergencies and for when you'll be venturing farther, two anchors and at least three hundred feet of line for each one are more realistic.

Any drifting after casting anchor, you'll discover, can generally be checked by one of these tactics. Just giving the rope a sudden tug often engages a dragging or slipping fluke with the bottom. You can sometimes accomplish the same thing by paying out more line, thus bettering the angle. If neither works, it's generally a matter of pulling up and beginning over, since distances between stable and uncertain anchorages frequently are only feet apart.

Weedy and rocky undersurfaces give the most trouble. There the heavier anchors are better, which is another justification for shipping more than a single. Such bottoms are commonly shown on charts, which is one more persuasion to heed those marine maps rather than haphazardly sail blithely and blindly.

MAN OR WOMAN OVERBOARD

Sailboat booms are for the most part so low that just during the sudden swings associated with jibing and tacking they're constantly challenging everybody aboard. This includes those sitting or lounging who, not alerted by the helmsman, don't have enough time to duck. This is additional reason for constant readiness to handle any problems of going over the side.

The lone skipper unexpectedly in the chop may see his craft, the wind ballooning her sails, nimbly scudding out of reach. Even a strong swimmer then can be in very real trouble without a lifeline, more common during transoceanic adventures, or one of the personal flotation provisions considered in connection with canoeing and sensible on deep water everywhere.

The passenger overboard will ordinarily be tossed a buoyant cushion or something better, then steered for until within reach. Although winds and currents create their own situations, such a rescue is most commonly accomplished by heading about a boat length downwind of the passenger overboard. Then just before reaching that target, angle directly toward him. This is usually easier when watch can be maintained over the side rather than the bow.

An upwind approach has to be handled much more precisely. Then the craft will be blown downwind at often a far greater speed than the swimmer, with the increased hazard of hitting whoever is in the water.

If sailing close-hauled at the time of the accident, you'll probably find safest turning with all speed to a beam reach. That way you'll be moving away from the swimmer for the several boat lengths necessary for maneuvering, whereupon you can jibe back and begin the same basic pattern.

If you're sailing on a beam reach, it will generally be well to keep on that course until far enough from the person overboard to turn and

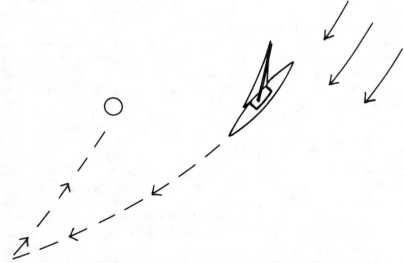

Figure 24. To rescue a man overboard, head downwind until you can angle upwind directly toward him.

make the other moves. Sailing on a broad reach usually makes it a matter of changing course to a beam reach and proceeding from that.

Tactics from a run are similar to those made from a beam reach, except that the turn is lengthier and the sail has to come in from a deeper set before the necessary beam reach is attained. The swimmer then will be upwind. Your next move, therefore, will be to tack instead of jibe.

Practice increases safety. Just dropping the occasional milk carton overboard in different situations, then experimenting in recovering it, can mean that one day you or someone else will be clambering back on board smiling.

Especially in water so cold it immobilizes with startling swiftness, the throwable flotation devices in which the swimmer can secure himself while enough strength remains also increase safety.

THE INTRIGUE OF SAILBOAT CONTROL

The breeze-driven craft are so vulnerable to being slowed and even stopped by such everyday phenomena as wind, current, and weather that it is only logical never to cast off for any extended sail without first making known your plans. This holds true even when the best you can do is leave a note somewhere reasonably prominent. Such procedure is a backup axiomatic with all travel of any sort in the unpeopled places, like the message wedged in a cleft branch before you leave an emergency shelter.

Control of the skittish sailboat at any time is so interlocked with immediate safety that, at least until you're well along to being an old hand, if your boat seems to be getting away, the best thing you usually can do is get canvas and anchor down until you can figure the next maneuver.

The difficulty may be nothing more than a local current faster than the wind, motive enough if you're planning very much sailing to become reasonably familiar with beckoning waters.

Such intimacy is often intriguingly achievable amid the pleasantries of charts, local tide tables (although not the so-called tide clocks), weather reports, and everywhere the pleasure of yarning with old-timers.

Chapter 21

High Safety

The secret you discover when continuing to walk long distances through the woods is never to step on anything you can step over, and never to step over anything you can step around. In climbing, it's never to use your knees for purchase where you can use your feet.

Here the safety margin lies even more in balance, born in some and acquirable by others. The mountaineer's legs provide much of the muscle. The arms and hands help position your weight over your feet, at the changing angles most advantageously coordinating your higher and higher holds.

The purest achievement of balance in the tall places is in friction climbing. Here, in harmony with momentum, the resistance to relative motion between the two entities—that is, the friction between your body and the rock—prevents a fall.

Before you reach this stage, slopes are so many and varied that as long as your motive remains pleasure, difficulty can be safely moderated in line with increasing ability. Even the blind have succeeded safely and enjoyably in climbing and descending Mount Rainier.

Nearly everyone with the desire can become a successful climber. This is particularly true as, short of ice and snow, all you need to start is rubber soles and whatever clothes may be sufficient for the local weather.

ROTE OF THE ROPE

The rope of even the tyro, when he or she keeps answering the lure of the high places, soon takes its place as a lifeline. It becomes a possession to be zealously guarded from sharp edges, dampness, kinking, and the consequences of being stepped on unnecessarily or dragged in the dust.

Before long you will be making sure that between climbs it's kept coiled, dry, safe from stray caustics, and whenever possible away from the deteriorative influence of sunlight and excessive heat. Before each ascent you'll be running the rope searchingly through your fingers, so as to find in time any localized roughness or discoloration that could spell weakness.

When the line no longer is prime, perhaps because of strain in checking a fall, you are likely to be experienced enough to sense the appropriateness of perhaps even giving it a place among your memorabilia, or at the least honorable retirement.

Needed knots will usually become so familiar in the meantime, in my case during the fun of odd-hour fiddling, that you'll be able to tie them swiftly and surely by feel alone. What I long carried for such pleasant practicing was a short length of twine.

PITON PRECAUTIONS

A major stay-safe habit with pitons is, whenever possible, placing each so that any fall will not end in a solid landing.

Then there's the listening as every piton is driven. Successively higher pitched rings confirm both the metal's and the rock's stability, as well as the firm union of crack and hardware. A dullness or hollowness to the hammer taps warns the piton may not be sound. When the weakness also is in the rock, the solution may be grouping several such supports.

Because pitons should go in hard all the way to the eye whenever possible, they are subjected to such stress that metal fatigue likely will become an increasing concern. Partly for this reason, although during a climb a needed piton may be hammered back into shape on the spot, blacksmithing at a later opportunity is preferable.

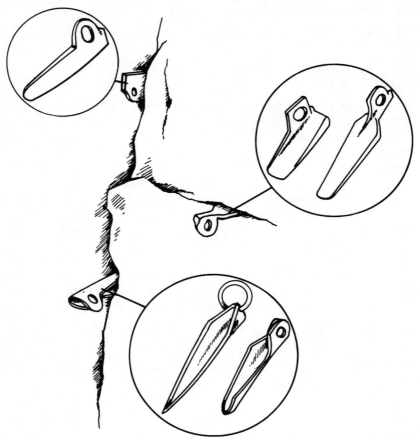

Figure 25. Pitons are metal spikes with an eye in the head to be driven into rock cracks and secure a climber's rope.

Reforming the metal cold tends to set up cracking. Such flaws appear most frequently at the vulnerable junction of shaft and head. Even though heat may leave the hardware slightly less strong, misshapen pitons as a whole can be more soundly restored with the help of anvil and forge.

A few hammer blows during the climb are the handiest way to keep the tips even. Any jaggedness or unsafe sharpness, generally appearing at the corners, is most easily smoothed routinely by abrasive stone or by file.

FIRST CLIMBING FIRST

The initial challenge of climbing first can often be answered more safely by strategic piton placements, always with the belayer's knowledge, along your lone way.

At the beginning, the unaccustomed drag of the rope, the added pull when a crack impedes its flow, and the sudden check then increasingly likely can become less formidable because the distance of any fall will be limited by the closest piton. The tumble, otherwise, would be at least twice as far as where whoever below is handling the rope.

BELAYING SAFETY

For everyone's safety, the beginner initially taking the belaying position may well self-anchor to a spur, bush, or piton once a vantage is found where, ideally, it will be possible to sit with feet braced and hands free to handle the rope.

Here, if you'll loop the rope around your hips so as to take advantage of friction, the ease with which you can control the weight below with one hand, while your other hand directs the slack, can be most pleasantly reassuring.

All this works, because belaying is a double act. The top performer, while smoothly keeping the routine taut, also watches the loose rope that's accumulating in the wings so that it won't dislodge such props as scree, or gather where it might snare or entangle you in an emergency.

The role of the second performer is to keep the rope from wedging and snagging, and to guard against any endangering tendencies invisible from above.

Vocal cues are best arranged beforehand. They should be simple, clear, and unlikely to be confused with those of some other climb. A life or death matter in any steep work can be the understanding that no one will take for granted that any signal has been heard and understood, but whenever possible will await a confirming reply.

RISK-LESSENED RAPPELLING

The rites of the rappel—descending by means of a doubled rope passed under one thigh, across the body, and over the opposite shoulder—are similar to those of the circus equestrian, in that both are best learned with a safe belay.

Later, staying ready to dodge the best you can when the retrieved line snakes downward will keep you better positioned to elude a whipping end.

A brisk, steady pull will usually free everything most handily. If the rope does jam, any dependence on the hung-up length in a last-resort salvaging ascent can abruptly bring real trouble. Settling for as much of the line as you can cut loose after reasonably climbing free is almost always the odds-on choice.

Jamming generally may be prevented where you can safely loop your rope around a bush or tree rather than tieing off around a rock spur or such. There also will be less chance then of abrasion damage.

Another safer anchor, when it can be maneuvered, starts with a small loop of expendable line, particularly when the climbing rope run through it hangs free. Pitons, on occasion placed below the rim, will also do.

THE FALLING STONES

Falling rock remains a danger throughout some ascents, particularly on roped climbs when it becomes necessary to follow a common route. Then especially, safety lies in watching, listening, and whenever possible hugging the incline.

Testing each hold more cautiously as you join in and endeavoring to avoid stone dislodgement by the rope itself will lessen risk. Some add the precaution of protective headgear.

Upon hearing or seeing a rock coming, or being alerted to it by a shout, safety can depend on last-moment ducking, leaning, squeezing, and in some situations flattening yourself against a sheer face.

RETREATING AND LIVING TO RETIRE

Turning back can mean returning safe, as when weather or route imposes unreasonable difficulties. The most frequent trouble, however, comes with darkness.

Because the time to the top is underestimated, night may close in before the target is reached. This is why old hands sometimes start up in the moonlight of pre-dawn. When melting snow and ice seem likely to accompany the sun, climbing on occasion begins its challenge as early as midnight.

Before any retreat is commenced, two considerations should be carefully analyzed. One is that a descent can be expected to take half as much time as the ascent. The other is that the way to the top may indeed be safer and shorter.

Despite the gravity difference, descents are usually trickier in places than going up. Facing outwards can reduce the difficulties. Even coming down at least sideways can better your chances of locating safe supports below. When you do have to face the rock, the safest procedure is supplementing feeling with frequent glances just beneath.

WHEN DARKNESS CLOSES IN

Once darkness obscures the face, both roped climbing and rappelling can become so hazardous that unless the distance remaining is relatively easy, your soundest maneuver is anchoring to the likeliest vantage. Ideally this will be at least a ledge wide enough to rest on comfortably until dawn.

Even when you succeed in relaxing enough to drowse, your refuge may be so cramped that you will have to resume your progress before you're once more limber. This is always an interval for extraordinary caution.

THE MOST TREACHEROUS TIME

An even more treacherous time is when you are coming down after a successful climb, especially one that has been difficult.

It's during such returns that accidents are most numerous. Combined during these anticlimaxes with understandable euphoria, relief, overconfidence, and slackening attention are frequently such other complications as deepening cold and dimness. Fatigue underlies everything almost always, along with the compulsion to get back to where there's shelter and something hot to eat and drink.

Chapter 22

What the Danger Really Is

Perils of being sucked into bottomless morasses abound in folklore, rather than in any swamps, marshes, quagmires, and mudflats you'll encounter.

In real life the only influence lying in wait is gravity whose force is felt, often abruptly, when you step wherever ground, decomposing vegetation, or both are mingled with water in proportions not stable enough to support your weight.

The moment anyone is enmired to the point where his body is no heavier than the semisolid it is displacing, he stops sinking. He does unless, perhaps panicking, he worms himself deeper in ineffectual struggling to get away.

Escape takes getting enough body area on the unstable surface to support your weight until you can get out, a choice depending in part on speed.

If when first sensing trouble you can reach firm underfooting by running, do so. Otherwise, dropping to your knees will often provide the means out. If not, without wasting time look for a branch, bush, or hummock to grab. Or you may have a jacket or packsack that can help sustain your weight. Otherwise, flatten yourself, with arms and when possible legs spread wide, and crawl.

Such unstable areas are encountered from high mountains to low flats. Wherever there is surface water, and especially where there was, is suspect.

It's well to remain wary when traveling across muskegs, swamps, marshes, tundra, and particularly the occasional animal lick which quivers beneath a masquerade of hardened mud. Once I almost lost a saddle horse in one, when she spooked off a game trail into the middle of unstableness.

Whenever stranded by outgoing tide on a strange, lone coastal flat, as while fishing or duck hunting, it's often simplest to stay with the boat.

QUICKSAND CAN BE QUICKER

Similar to quagmires, being granules suspended in water, quicksand can drop you even quicker. Although the escape tactics are the same, they generally must be swifter. It's often even more essential to keep free of sudden unreasoning terror.

Unless support or assistance is at hand, the way out frequently lies in flinging yourself flat and then crawling or swimming clear. Initially you may have to duck to free your feet, loosening them by hand and if necessary unhesitatingly sacrificing your boots or shoes. In any event, avoid unnecessarily violent movement that would only force you deeper.

If exhaustion interrupts, rest, but never give up. Quicksand as well as quagmires commonly occupy areas whose surfaces are no larger than a living room sofa.

EXPECT TO FALL

When just walking through the woods a reasonable precaution is continually gauging, consciously until it becomes second nature, where and how if you fall, you'll be able to land most safely. Soundly testing any handholds below, as when you're descending a rocky bank, can prevent severe trouble—unless you happen to be lucky. One time far from habitation I fell head first when part of a familiar undercut ledge which I didn't bother to examine first crumbled beneath my weight-supporting palm.

Deadfall which cannot be reasonably circumvented is another danger. This one wetness multiplies, especially when its presence and consequences are unsuspected. Just dew or frost can make a bare log so slippery that, short of help from caulked footwear, your control is instantly gone.

Neither cleats nor the usual spikes provide any protection when dead bark turns up unexpectedly on a fallen trunk.

Proceeding with appropriate caution everywhere, particularly when you're on your own, can go a long way toward ensuring a lifetime of accident-free wilderness travel, actually simplest in the most primitive places.

WAYS OF SAFER WALKING

Where there are long distances to cover, walking as much as possible with the toes straight ahead, as the pioneers found the Indians doing, has proved most productive. This is especially evident when you can land on your heel and ride forward to the ball of your foot with steady, easy, springy steps.

Any toeing-out puts added stress on the knees, particularly when you quicken into a run or otherwise press to make time. At best, toeing-out demands that these joints work differently from the way they were designed. Since mankind began walking upright, anyway, each foot has been supporting double the weight for which it seemingly was devised.

Just changing your socks at least once during the day, and preferably again when you make camp, can make all this physically easier. It can help as well to keep disabling skin irritation and even infection from starting.

A practical ruse in much wild country is carrying a hotel-size cake of soap and one extra set of hose, then washing the worn pair when freshwater appears beside the trail, hanging them on your pack or belt to dry.

In cold streams, the wool you'll be better off wearing responds well to soap if your washing is not overstrenuous and the socks are pressed free of water rather than wrung, then allowed to dry slowly. Detergents extract natural oils from these animal fibers, and they should be avoided. If no soap is available, just a swish and then a rinse will be better.

STARTING EARLY TO BE SAFE LATER

The greatest percentage of serious injuries involve feet and ankles, especially when hurrying is involved. Some of these disabilities are set up unnecessarily during the formative public high school years.

Such crippling infirmities in later life as arthritis, Dr. James A. Nicholas, director and founder of the Institute of Sports Medicine and Athletic Trauma at the Lenox Hill Hospital in New York, has concluded are still being triggered by needless sports injuries. Some of these injuries result from adolescents being grouped by age rather than by physical differences.

NEEDLESS KNEE DIFFICULTIES

The most common and serious of these early impairments are in the knee. Kneecap injuries, more frequent among females, many times are patterned during the group recreational sports these girls are being included in between the ages of twelve and eighteen, and in which they have sometimes been started while too immature.

One sign of kneecap or patellar instability in young people is an inability to sit still for long without extending their legs.

Girls with this overall problem begin, long before any indications show up in physical examinations and X rays, to develop pain during gymnastics and on occasion during dancing classes. Untreated Jumper's Knee, a common name for patella tendon strain, can become debilitating and psychologically devastating for those who want to continue dancing, if only in the ballroom.

Young girls with such instability, Dr. Nicholas believes, should discontinue all jumping sports for two to three years during the course of maturing, while pubic hair grows into its normal distribution pattern and full height is reached.

As maturing occurs, the elongating effect on the patella tendon diminishes. Rotation tends to be lessened as, along with depth and width development of the joint surfaces, laxity decreases and strength grows.

"Successful treatment depends on rest of the affected area from bending or rotating," suggests this physician for a number of New York's bigger professional teams. "It should be done without splints or plaster casts that lead to further wasting of the already weakened thigh."

Doctor Nicholas prescribes a sitting exercise to restore thigh flexion: raise the foot ten to twenty times periodically without extending the knee with the help of a suspended weight.

Another feminine leg problem may be later arthritic difficulty caused by softened cartilage, a condition called chondromalacia, and arising from dislocations on the undersurface of the kneecap. In many instances this condition is self-limiting, at least to the extent that it does not reassert itself until menopause, especially when the older woman is active in a strenuous sport.

Chapter 23

Sidestepping the Mechanical Menaces

Camping ranks third in popularity among this country's outdoor recreations in which there is individual participation. It is led only by swimming and cycling and is well ahead of fishing and boating, according to a Nielsen survey. The average time spent camping each year by the so inclined American family is just under seventeen days.

Of the camping households examined, 31.8 percent own a recreational vehicle. More Americans, with more and more leisure and means to join the surge toward participator sports, are heading for open country in motor homes and pickup campers.

Not all are successful in reaching their destination safely. Many of the motor homes are big, high, and wide. The also unfamiliar height and configuration of the average slide-in campers make them susceptible, when not operated with adequate safety, to tipping over in a turn. Both of these vehicles have significantly more weight than the usual present-day recreationist is accustomed to controlling when changing lanes, passing, and gravitating downgrade with building momentum.

Overloading and improper stowing in this sort of outdoor travel also continue to set up accidents, largely the result of stability and maneuvering problems, suspension system failures, and unanticipated difficulties encountered during emergency stops.

Practice and the owner manuals, along with preventive maintenance and most of all common sense, can make such camping excursions more uniformly enjoyable.

NEEDLESS CARBON MONOXIDE POISONING

Carbon monoxide poisoning, especially with the slide-in campers, is unwarrantedly high in the safety statistics. One cause of such killer conditions, considered in more detail in Chapter 26, is installing the unit without making sure the vehicle's tailpipe extends beyond both it and the added overhang, or sidewise, safely into the airstream.

Otherwise, any flooring leakage can let in a lethal flow of exhaust fumes, which any sleeping passengers may not wake up to smell.

As an added precaution, rear doors and windows customarily are best kept shut while traveling. Too, the more fully equipped combinations with accessories such as air conditioners and heaters operated by the vehicle's engine, may in some cases be outfitted more advantageously by providing a separate and safer secondary source of power.

FIRES ON THE ROAD

Vigilance alone can circumvent many of the sort of fires and explosions still occurring among the camping conveyances with LP (liquid petroleum) gas systems. An odor of onions or garlic can be enough of a tip-off that there is a leak, if one keeps the possibility in mind.

Heavy soapy water smeared over suspect joints often is a practical way to locate such leakage safely. In the meantime, any smoking will be less risky somewhere else. Even turning electrical switches on and off is best avoided until all is tight.

At a service station pump during refueling just a lit pilot light can trigger an explosion.

A smoke detector operated by its own battery can wake sleepers in time when fire starts in the wiring system. Then a fire extinguisher, such as one of today's foam-mist types, may be all that will be needed to quell it. Carrying two extinguishers, one in the cab and one in the living quarters, provides markedly better protection in a pickup camper; in a motor home, carry one toward the front and the other where it can be handily reached at the back.

On the road in a dual-wheel motor home, also be alert for tire fires resulting from undetected flats.

SAFER TRAILERING

When safety chains are used—along with a breakaway switch for activating the separate braking system (that's required in many states for loaded trailers weighing more than a thousand pounds) in case of hitching-mechanism failure—crossing this chain under the trailer tongue with enough slack can keep the tongue from ever dropping and digging dangerously into the roadway.

With the electric brakes currently most widely used with boat trailers, there's the added hazard that the electrical system will be damaged when the vehicle is backed into the water for unloading. This is a reason many boat trailers are equipped with surge brakes. But these can bring their own problems. One is a lack of simultaneous braking action on the towing and towed vehicles, without provision for separate controlled activation. Another is too heavy tongue weight that can leave the brakes inoperative.

A light hitch load, on the other hand, may cause the trailer to fishtail in ratio with weight and speed. Conversely, too hefty a hitch load, in addition to overburdening the towing vehicle, can bring about touchy steering, faulty cornering, and undependable braking capability.

The manufacturer's manual, as well as any trailering guide for the vehicle used in pulling, can help make journeying with the already convenient boat and camping trailers safe. This becomes particularly true when their information is accompanied by systematic self-training with the techniques and the individualities of your particular combination.

Then it's mostly a matter of keeping the extra weight in mind, along with the realization that most trailering accidents occur when the trailer starts pushing the towing vehicle downhill.

Chapter 24

The Challenge of Cycling Control

HEAD LIGHT, TAIL LIGHT
SIDE REFLECTORS

America's most accident-ridden outdoor recreation continues to be cylcing, in part because of the higher-risk age groups that zoom the roads and the back country trails.

Even bike-with-bike collisions are common, pointing to the sense of having a visibility-expanding head beam, whether mandated by law or not. Also advisable is either a taillight or a reflective rear strip, so that approaching danger is less likely itself to be blind.

HEAD, FEET, AND HANDS

The motorcycle's agility and maneuverability, along with its singular ability to stop suddenly or swerve swiftly off the pavement, are advantages you can capitalize on to offset what you have to give up in weight, bulk, and other built-in protection for such nimbleness.

Skill in these maneuvers can be enough, even while you're sharpening it more, to keep you from joining the statistics which still show that four out of every five reported motorcycle accidents result in injury or death. (With automobiles it is one in five.) Motorcycle deaths are double those of other vehicles.

Controlling expanded visibility can be your most important offensive, especially at intersections where the majority of motorcycle-automobile collisions occur. A pivotal part is anticipation, both of what may be underneath and what may be ahead.

Your clothing can offer still more protection when it takes into account those parts of the body most often injured: the arms, legs, and most dangerously the head.

Leather or heavy denim sleeves reduce the likelihood of abrasions in the event of a spill. So do leather gloves, as well as the special fabric types with leather palms and leather strips along the fingers, which are an answer to the safety essential of maintaining a sure grip.

Functional leather boots are most dependable if you're going to stay in charge. The right rugged shoes, which cover the ankle, are probably your safest second choice. Sneakers, sandals, and similar light wear do not protect the feet adequately from friction or from the crushing that can happen in encounters with trees, rocks, and the other natural impediments often brushed against while bucking unfrequented trails.

Goggles, glasses, and the helmets with face shields can assure uninterrupted sight when they are shatterproof, scratchproof, and ventilated well enough to do away with any fog buildup. Although tints can enhance specific daylight conditions, clear night lenses are most practical.

The critical choice remains the helmet. The symbol *DOT* on the outer rear surface of those in the medium-to-large range, which is presently covered by federal safety standards, indicates the manufacturer's certification of conformity.

With the small and the extra-large helmets, a label inside showing approval by SHCA (Safety Helmet Council of America) or SNELL (Snell Memorial Foundation) carries these organizations' assurances of quality. Some helmets with the SNELL qualification, however, are intended only for off-road wear.

PARTICULAR PERIL

Wherever other drivers being able to see you may be a decisive safety factor, your daytime cycling clothing should include orange or at least some nearly comparable eye-alerting color like red, better still when florescent.

Reflective material on vehicle and garb, including the helmet, help to make riders more noticeable at night, the witching hours when even surface conditions that are only irritating to motorists become for the two-wheeled cyclers increasingly hazardous.

A danger spot at any time on curving two-lane roads is just behind the left rear fender, or on occasion the right, of a fast-moving automobile whose driver cannot see the motorcyclist who is ready to pass. One harrowing situation is when, by the time the car driver suddenly realizes the cyclist is alongside, fast traffic is closing from the other direction and neither driver knows whether to accelerate or brake. Traveling with motorcycle headlights on day and night, sound practice wherever there is traffic, sets up at least alerting reflections for the automobilist in such blind-spot crises.

IV

AUTUMN

Fear had taught me to move noiselessly, to climb trees, to pinpoint sound, and now in order to penetrate into the deepest recesses and enjoy the best in nature, it was essential to learn how to use my eyes and my rifle.

Jim Corbett

Chapter 25

Campfires and Autumn Lightning

The meagerness of the risk combined with the awesomeness of wind-scoured summits can make them agreeably stimulating, especially after only prudent precautions. But when autumn thunderstorms rumble above the high peaks and exposed ridges of sheep and goat country, climbers are in enough danger to be concerned.

The ridges encourage development of the vertical updrafts and the rain cloud formations which generate lightning. The mountaintops help actuate the strokes. Even the surrounding air, usually a good insulator, ionizes in the company of so much electrical stress and becomes a conductor.

Yet if you huddle fifty feet below such heights, and from ten to fifty feet away from the rock face, you will be in the safety zone. Closer to the mountainside, you may become an alternate route for a bolt. Seeking protection under an overhang can be even more hazardous. There you'd be setting yourself up as a potential lightning rod.

Small caves give similar false assurance. Ideally, any refuge will be deep and broad enough for you to sit at least the length of your body away from the walls. Any roof should be at least ten times your

140 In lightning stay away from rock faces, overhangs, small caves. a big cave 12^3 feet is o.k.

height at the moment—standing, sitting, or whatever. You will still do well to keep away from the front, across which lightning may jump.

The more compact your position the safer, for this will shorten the span of your contact points with rock or ground. Neither your especially vulnerable head nor your torso should be included in any span, as would happen if you sprawled with shoulders against the wall.

Sitting wholly, feet and all, on some insulator such as a dry jacket or coiled rope will minimize the risk even more. Just crouching on a loose slab or boulder will help.

CAUGHT ON SHEER ROCK

The more insidious peril, when an electric storm catches you climbing on sheer rock, lies in the earth currents then involved. Just their sudden sting on feet and hands can disrupt balance and even cause a lost hold. Higher voltages can cause muscle spasms, sometimes unconsciousness.

Often a sound precaution, for a beginner in particular, is to tie on. The shorter the distance to such an anchor point, the less the voltage gradient along the rope will be. Nylon line, rather than the older fibers such as manila, will reduce the potential further.

Climbing metal does not attract electricity to any significant degree, reason enough for never making the sometimes disastrous mistake of discarding pitons, crampons, ice axes, and such. The electrical resistance of the usual ice axe is far greater than that of the human body. Even the slightly offsetting effects of dampening wood can be countered beforehand by wax or linseed oil.

Rappelling out of the danger zone may be worth the calculated risk of being dislodged en route by a shock. Three things will narrow even this possibility of becoming a lightning statistic: dryness, nylon rope, and rapid descent with only the close-together feet ever touching the rock.

THE DANGER IN AFTERSHOCK

The crackling of a corona or its nearby bluish glow, known to some as Saint Elmo's Fire, are alerts well to heed when thunderclouds are close.

Such phenomena do not necessarily imply peril, although your hair may begin to sputter and even to stand on end. Nevertheless, they are the result of electrically overstressed air which has become a ready lightning conductor.

The atmospheric charges may have been left by clouds since evaporated. But even the involuntary contraction of an arm or leg muscle, induced by an unexpected shock from what accumulation may be lingering and too light to be of consequence elsewhere, may be enough to disorder an already precarious equilibrium or hold.

MEANWHILE, BACK AT CAMP

When night after night the geese come lumbering in with a clangor and a whistling of wings, even after the lake by your base camp begins skimming with ice, collecting dead wood for your campfire becomes all the more urgent. So, unless you've a liquid fuel stove or the like, does wigwaming the kindling each time and once again getting it lighted.

If one method does not succeed, there is always another. But the realization that this first flicker of flame is often elusive, to be won only arduously, becomes all the more reason to acquire such skill before the decisive moment when it can make the difference.

The ability seems to come best a bit at a time over a long period, when on each occasion you use only whatever native materials may be at hand, especially those which can be expected to be still available the perhaps snow-bitten night when a campfire may be your turning point. One thing most of us learn along the outdoor ways is that it is far more satisfactory to deal with natural difficulties by adaption or avoidance, rather than by attempting to overcome them by force.

WHAT ACTUALLY BURNS

Although campfires can be built countless ways, they always proceed from spark, to tinder, to fuel. The wood itself does not burn, but rather the gas driven from it by heat. The flame in turn must be kept hot enough to light the more and more gas that, in combination with the oxygen in the air, is generated from progressively larger amounts of fuel.

Knowing this, enjoying campfires in every sort of weather becomes a whole lot simpler. All you need carry is, ideally, a small waterproof and preferably breakproof container filled with strike-anywhere wooden matches.

Anyone who lets himself or herself become dependent on any of the commercial fire-starting aids risks needing a warm blaze one chill dusk when they're without an artificial booster and not having the experience to get a fire going.

Such manufactured starters, far from being what some advertisers call indispensable musts for everyone traveling outdoors, can be endangering as well as needless burdens, expenses, and bothers. Coming to rely on always having one, instead of learning nature's fundamentals, can get you killed.

THE METAL MATCH

The so-called Metal Match, which only provides a spark, can be a practical backup to keep stowed in a pocket in case your regular matches ever run out. There it should be kept adequately covered, both to protect it from efficiency-diminishing body oil and from prolonged exposure to humidity which will eventually decompose it into gray dust.

Compounded from what are described as eleven rare earth metals, extruded in very high temperature from inert gases, the Metal Match is fireproof, nontoxic, to a major extent waterproof, and reasonably durable. Depending on its size you can quickly and simply light with it between some one thousand and three thousand fires.

Just shave several small bits from it with the back of a knife or with even a sharp stone. The fragments, compactly grouped amid tinder, can be ignited by the spark a swift, downward sweep along the match by the same knife back or keen stone will produce. Although such sparks embody heat as high as 2,800°F., these last so briefly that the Metal Match can be safe in inexperienced hands.

LIGHTING THE LITTLE FIRES

A practical way to get your campfire started in conifer country is by lighting a fistful of the small dead resinous twigs which abound dryly underneath pines and other evergreens, even when the rest of the forest is sheeted with ice.

First grouping on clear ground a few shreds of birch bark, harmlessly pulled from the trunks on which scores loosely flutter, can speed even this basic technique. The bark's inherent oil urges its pronging with flames even when wet. These lift into the resin-rich twigs massed atop, loosely enough for ventilation.

Small dry sticks broken from the same standing softwoods then may be angled and crisscrossed over the blazing nucleus. In blusterous weather when the wind is abroad, having them already piled can make everything surer. Afterward, it's just a matter of feeding your little fire with the larger stuff.

BREAKING THROUGH THAT ICE

Depending on the country and on whether or not you have even a skeletonized Hudson's Bay ax with which to chop a nearer hole, getting water for drinking and cooking sometimes leads to venturing farther from shore than the perhaps still too thin ice will support you.

Then once out of even shallow icy water, if everything happens rapidly enough, rolling in dry snow can blot up much of the moisture before it reaches your body. Any dampness remaining will in really frigid weather freeze almost immediately, and its resulting armor provide a makeshift windbreaker while you're getting back to your campfire.

Chapter 26

Tinders, Fuels, and Fumes

Since man and woman first groped out of the cold caves, almost limitless tinders, so combustible that a spark in them can be blown to flame, have helped them start fires.

A handful of powder-dry evergreen needles, rubbed and broken together, is in this age-old group. So are the sometimes more available dry bat droppings, dead grasses (especially witch's hair), bark from certain cedars, and the tops of Arctic cotton grass, all also when pulverized.

Dried mushrooms and other fungi, as well as crisp lichen and moss, can be readied this way for beginning campfires, as can wood dry-rotted enough to be powdered. The fine dust insects produce under the moisture-excluding bark of dead trees is suitable as is. Indians collected the dried pith found inside elderberry shoots for this purpose, as they did the down that beds many wild nests, including those of the field mice.

The down in the under portions of waterfowl and other birds sought for food, along with the finer feathers also serves. Floss from such edible plants as firewood and milkweed is effective, too, as is the fluffiness of the eminently edible cattail and the pussy willow. Even the edible giant puffball has dry spongy threads which make excellent tinder.

BEYOND TIMBERLINE

Driftwood sometimes is the only readily available fuel. In far northern regions where there is not even this, peat and coal occasionally abound on the surface. The small heather-like evergreen there, called cassiope, will burn even when green and wet. Brush and roots can usually be found, and there are the moss and lichens seasonally beneath the snow.

Above timberline in the mountains and the high latitudes, there are commonly enough stunted bushes for campfires. On the plains also there is the small vegetation, along with roots such as those of the mesquite, grass to knot into bundles, and the desiccated cattle refuse which has taken the place of the buffalo chips.

HEATS AND WOODS

Although the conifers' softwoods make starting a campfire easier, the denser hardwoods keep it burning steadier and longer. The water content of both, greatest when the growth is living or has been lying long on damp ground, is an even more important factor. Unless you want smoke, trying to start a fire with wood that has been lying on damp ground generally is a waste of time.

Although even the greenest wood will burn if there is enough heat and time, it's the dry sticks, along with such exceptions as living ash and birch, that quickly get the bright small blazes crackling.

Taking all this into account, your best offhand guide is weight. The more heft, the more heat.

In back country it is a matter of doing the best you can with what is at hand, but when there's a choice some knowledge of comparative input-output relative to heat may help.

The woods giving the most warmth, one cord roughly equaling one ton of anthracite coal, are in order: apple, American beech, rock elm, butternut hickory, shagnut hickory, ironwood, black locust, and white oak.

Next in line, a cord approximately equivalent to nine-tenths of a ton of the hard coal, are: white ash, white birch, yellow birch, black cherry, sugar maple, red oak, and black walnut.

Following in order, with one cord affording about as much warmth as eight-tenths of a ton of anthracite, are: black ash, green ash, American elm, red maple, silver maple, pitch pine, American sycamore, and tamarack of Eastern larch.

The scale continues downward, the heat equivalent of a cord of wood to six-tenths of a ton of the coal, from aspen, basswood, butternut, balsam fir, hemlock, red pine, white pine, and red spruce to black willow.

pine gives good light, however

SOLID TROUBLES WITH LIQUID FUELS

More and more, a lot of what's still called camping is becoming big business. A recent survey by the Coleman Company shows that 45 to 55 percent of all Americans have camped within the past three years or are interested in camping in the near future.

Liquid fuel burners and stoves, very useful in some areas and mandatory in many, are now among the official equipment of the Boy Scouts of America who not too long ago stressed, instead, the importance of lighting a campfire with never more than two matches.

Anything less than clean and reasonably fresh white gas in today's gasoline lanterns, stoves, and catalytic heaters generally leads to trouble. Unleaded gasolines contain additives that eventually clog generators on the camp stoves and lanterns, necessitating if you use them much repeated cleaning or replacing unless someone surrenders and junks them. The additives eventually coat the wicks of catalytic heaters sufficiently to leave them useless.

All gasolines ordinarily pumped at filling stations can permanently damage catalytic heaters. The regular and the traditional ethyl-enhanced premium grades, deposit alien lead compounds.

As for pouring the petroleum naphtha from your campground stove into your motor vehicle's depleted gas tank, it may get you back on the road. But the more intense heat generated during combustion and the absence of the additives common to present automobile fuels frequently bring about dieseling. Car engines tend to continue running after the ignition key is turned off. Knocking can also be caused, and pistons and valves damaged.

Any liquid fuel left during the winter in camp stoves and lanterns should be safely dumped and replaced with fresh in the spring. Then when your salivary glands are working and you want heat in a hurry to broil fresh trout, or enough light to watch their sizzling progress, dinner won't be stalled by condensation that's been building up in the tanks.

you can't dump this anywhere w/o hurting the environment!

Campers, as well as hunting and fishing enthusiasts, get into the

store air-tight in fall.

habit of innovating. When this is directed toward modifying and individualizing portable stoves and lights, too often the air flow essential to proper operation is at best unbalanced, sometimes perilously, so that overheating and even leaking may occur.

VITAL VENTILATION

Like people, other fuel-burning mechanisms consume oxygen from the air. They emit carbon dioxide, water vapor, unused hydrocarbons, and carbon monoxide. Adequate ventilation is everywhere necessary to replace the oxygen and to rid the surrounding atmosphere of the emissions and by-products.

Small stoves, including the wood burners, kept going overnight in tents to ward off chill still cause fatalities when the pores in the fabric, unwisely depended on for adequate air circulation, are closed as by snow.

THE STEALTHY KILLER

Everyone knows the insidious carbon monoxide is odorless and invisible. Not so many realize this stealthy killer is cumulative. Small amounts breathed a few nights from an unsuspected tent stove, for instance, gradually build up in the body until the relatively miniscule quantity inhaled the next night means never awakening again.

Deepening cold heightens the hazard because of the natural reaction of decreasing ventilation to increase warmth. Those with an anemic condition suffer first and most, but with everyone there's usually not even any warning difficulty with breathing.

The always surrounding carbon dioxide in the atmosphere, once it is turned into carbon monoxide by half of its oxygen being taken away, has over the centuries, in new country especially, caused innumerable deaths long attributed to other causes.

The age-old problem of carbon monoxide poisoning worsened for a time with some of today's most modern structures as the result of misunderstandings about the natural quality of air in general, as well as efforts to save everyone's energy. One result has been that a number of "tighter buildings" inadvertently added to interior health and safety risks by trapping carbon monoxide, formaldehyde, radioactive radon, and other dangerous and, ironically, energy-wasting fumes.

PROBLEMS OF "OXYGEN OR ELSE"

Symptoms of carbon monoxide poisoning, when any are noticed, may start with tightening across the forehead, slight flushing, and headache which as exposure continues steadily becomes more acute. Dizziness, weakness, and difficulty seeing may become evident.

In severe cases, there's cherry-redness to nails, tissues, and such mucous membranes as those in the mouth. Nausea and vomiting may be followed by collapse. Thereupon pulse and breathing often quicken and respiration many times becomes labored and ragged. Sometimes, though, carbon monoxide poisoning proceeds only far enough to cause headache, digestive disturbances, and an inexplicable feeling of being unwell. Symptoms occasionally are chronic.

Relief intervened in time to save the life of Adm. Richard E. Byrd, isolated alone at his solitary weather station in the Antarctic night. During these five adventurous and productive months, he became exposed to carbon monoxide fumes as a result of faulty ventilation. By the time he became aware of what was happening, he was no longer strong enough to correct it.

If the others from his party back at Little America had not arrived a few minutes after midnight, coma likely would have come instead, convulsions followed, and heart and lung function slowed. Eventually, death probably would have overtaken him.

Fresh air commonly is the most immediate need with carbon monoxide poisoning, then warmth and quiet to decrease the body's oxygen requirements. In cases of unconsciousness, mouth-to-mouth resuscitation should be started as soon as possible. Because of the carbon dioxide content of the rescuer's breath, this is preferable to other artificial methods, including the use of oxygen.

Carbon monoxide, when it hasn't long been accumulating, tends to leave the body with encouraging quickness when its air intake is five to ten percent carbon dioxide. As soon as the victim is breathing on his or her own, carbon dioxide may be furnished by means of paper bags, or other suitable containers, into which a companion exhales. With several people producing these supplies, recovery can be speeded significantly.

Aftereffects may linger whatever is done, and throughout the victim should be watched so that you can treat, as well as you can, any reverses.

Chapter 27

The Wrong Fear

The kind of apprehension about wild animals that comes out panic instead of respect can get anyone in very real trouble. When the result is the inciting smell of terror, and certainly when it is the direct invitation to chase of running, the outcome is sometimes unnecessarily uncomfortable.

Actually, you are far safer in any untamed American and Canadian wilderness than during the travel it takes you to get there.

The widely dreaded timber wolves, for example, don't make the vicious onslaughts depicted in motion pictures and television entertainment and in other fiction. Wolves in the real wilds, rather than leaping overnight fires and attacking campers, exert their high order of intelligence never even to be glimpsed by a human being.

The only unprovoked wild animal in North America which is occasionally dangerous is the polar bear among the ice floes of the remote Arctic.

It is the once wild animals whose inborn wariness has been blunted by civilization who are no longer predictable. Among these are the tourist-fed bear in and around government parks such as Yellowstone. Some of these bear at one time inhabited such areas and in some

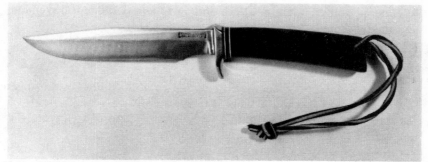

Figure 26. This custom "Angier Trail Knife," displayed in the Harvard Museum, is handmade by W. D. Randall with a straight 6-inch blade of the finest quality high carbon Swedish tool steel, designed for all around camp and trail, as well as boating. The top of the blade is notched for surer thumb placement.

instances were trapped or sedated and transported elsewhere, because through no fault of their own they had become potentially dangerous to the tourists.

THE PERIL IN BLUFFING

If you encounter a large animal who shows no inclination to leave, stay motionless. Too, talking in as calm, placid, and even lanquid a manner as you can has a soothing effect on wild animals. Any I have met in the open, if they didn't immediately sift into the surroundings, have regarded me briefly and in most instances then moved away, usually without any sign of undue concern or excitement.

You'll naturally get any firearm into position as casually and smoothly as possible, especially if the animal is at such close quarters that any abrupt move might provoke a similar reaction. However, it will seldom be wise to shoot. Appearing relaxed and only mildly interested averages out better. Best is when you have absorbed enough knowledge and experience to be really that way.

Never threaten unless you are ready to back it up or have a safe means of retreat. Bluffing brings a responding surge of adrenalin, which may be all the animal needs to go on the offensive. At best, threatening of any sort is apt to be countered by escalating concern. When a wild animal feels endangered, it instinctively seeks a way out of the situation. That way may be over you.

If the animal shows no indication of giving ground, you may prefer to leave yourself with, at the least, the semblance of as much indifference as you can summon, continuing to avoid sudden movements and talking quietly.

IF THIS DOES NOT WORK

If the moment does come when you decide to shoot—as has been forced upon me only once when I inadvertently cornered a moose in the narrowness of what I didn't know was a dead-end canyon—act unexpectedly, decisively, and with no warning shot.

Shoot to stop. A bullet that does not anchor but only kills, as in the heart, still leaves more than enough time for you to be killed, too. Head-on, a spine shot centered slightly below where the neck joins the body is quickest, except for one in the brain. To hit this smaller and better protected target, aim between and a bit over the eyes. The surest combined killer and stopper is the paralyzing, immobilizing, deadly shoulder shot in line with the forelegs, one-third of the way down an animal's body.

Not even the most deadly bullet fired from the highest caliber rifle is sure of killing big game in its tracks unless it strikes the brain or the frontal spinal column.

THE NECK SHOT

"The neck is where I like to connect," an old-timer told me once around Whitehorse when I was heading outside past Chilkoot Pass. "Mind you hit pretty nigh center, lest you miss the bone. Then you'll be eating beans awhile longer, except when you're only a mite low and cut the jugular vein."

That is pretty much the story of the much-touted neck shot, regarded among sourdoughs as a meat saver. You need to pick your spot, remembering while disregarding hair that the spinal column runs near the center of the neck. Frontally, a spine shot centered slightly below where the neck joins the body is more dependable, surpassed only by the trickier brain shot.

The eyes and ears indicate the position of the relatively small brain in big game. To reach it, aim at a spot which, from the side, is midway along an imaginary line between the eye and ear cavities. From the front, aim between and slightly above the eyes.

You can also reach the brain from behind. However, if you do choose to shoot from the rear at an uninjured animal, a more reasonable way is to aim as precisely as you can at the base of the tail, figuring on either missing cleanly or dropping the animal with a hit in the spine.

A bullet into the spinal column instantly paralyzes game. Unless forward of the shoulder, however, it may require a finishing shot.

If you need the meat so that you can keep going, of course go for the midbody. Quartering shots can be most effectively slanted to reach the region between the shoulders a little higher than midbody.

THE FIRST BULLET

The lung shot is deadly. The heart shot is seldom quicker, and when the lower portions of this organ are hit, it is not always so sudden. The killing shot affording the widest margin for error is one into the center of the chest.

An animal shot in the heart may drop instantly or run out of sight, sometimes more than a mile. When following the trail of big game that's been hit anywhere vital and taken off, ordinarily it's not productive to track farther than a couple of hundred yards for up to an hour.

Afterwards, if it isn't found dead, it will probably leave its bed stiffly enough for a sure finishing shot. Otherwise, you may never find it, despite the fact it probably will later die. This is a situation no sportsman or sportswoman ever wants to have happen, and especially not when there's the danger of its charging anyone unexpectedly and disastrously from cover.

The first bullet in most instances should do the job or it should not be taken. When you do shoot and the game doesn't drop, except perhaps in a survival situation when ammunition is limited, a sound rule is to continue aimed firing as long as the animal stands on its feet.

DEAD OR JUST STUNNED

Always it's well to approach an apparently dead animal with extreme caution, from the rear whenever possible. When you come fairly near, try throwing a stick, stone, or clump of dirt to see if it moves.

Many hunters have been seriously hurt and some killed when getting too close to the front of a downed animal they took for dead. Even members of the widely underrated deer family can inflict terrible wounds with antlers and deadly sharp hoofs.

Considerable trouble in the long run can be avoided by checking the eyes of apparently dead big game before committing yourself by advancing within its reach. One way is by kicking ground litter into an eye, another by touching it with a long stick. Using your gun barrel instead can result in the weapon's being knocked or wrenched away at the decisive moment you need it to stay unharmed, while accidental firing may add to the difficulties.

Another sensitive spot is the testicles.

Even when no response is apparent whatever you do, it is reasonable to remain wary of sharp feet, horns, or antlers until the major entrails are removed and, to a lesser extent, even afterward because of the threat remaining in possible reflex action.

Occasionally a hunter is seriously attacked when stooping to cut a presumably dead animal's throat. (This is done despite the facts that the unnecessary slash doesn't let enough blood escape to have any effect on the meat, and that often it spoils the neck skin for mounting.)

You soon learn to gut and dress a large animal at once, propping open its abdomen perhaps with a stick so the inside can air and cool. If you can't get the game to camp right away or move your camp to it, before you leave at least cover it loosely as with conifer boughs to keep the jays, whisky jacks, hawks, magpies, eagles, and their ilk from the meat, especially the nutritively vital fat.

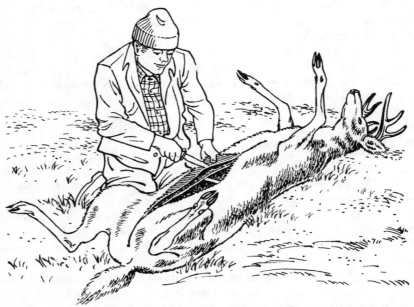

Figure 27. Cut an animal immediately after ascertaining that it is dead. Use a stick to prop open the abdomen so that it can air and cool.

CUTTING THROUGH RATHER THAN YOU

Safety with your hunting knife, W.D. "Bo" Randall (who with his son Gary has long hand made some of the best) suggests, is mainly a matter of thinking about being safe rather than fast.

Then even the northern Indian's habit of cutting toward one's self, although best avoided by most, remains harmless. Otherwise, it's easy for even a veteran hunter when he's butchering and skinning to slash steadying fingers, not always his own.

The sometimes high-spirited throwing is really a specialized sport calling for specially made knives. The sheath knife that may later save your life can be too easily damaged even if, glancing or bouncing, it does not hurt somebody or get lost.

The case in which the hunting knife is kept when not being used should be rugged enough and sufficiently well constructed that neither point nor cutting edge can injure the carrier, or the knife itself slip out.

A sharp blade is safer than a dull one. This is particularly true when you are depending on the effective sawing stroke rather than on pressure. Then the edge is more likely to cut where intended than to skid.

Keeping the edge keen by honing, although safe and easy when concentrated upon, can cause troublesome gashes, if not worse, when distractions interrupt. Carbon steel is more easily and satisfyingly kept sharp than stainless steel.

ANOTHER PART OF BEING READY

In game-rich country, keep your rifle safely handy and ready. I've gotten needed meat while boiling the noonday kettle, going for tea water, taking care of camp chores, once when saddling my horse to go hunting, and even when awakened in my sleeping bag by a moose treading on the tremulous ground about a lick during the long autumn dawn of the subarctic.

When your hobbled pack string is foraging where you camp, it's well to hang it in a tree safely away from the cayuses' hooves.

In a canoe, especially when rapids may be ahead, buckle the sling as well as the shoulder strap of the rucksack, with your spare ammunition and extra waterproof match case, around one of the thwarts. Then in the more remote places if you are unlucky or inept enough to have an upset, you'll at least have saved your rifle, cartridges, matches, and perhaps your life.

Vilhjalmur Stefansson, the Arctic explorer who lived there by his rifle alone for a dozen years, once told me an accident or "adventure" in the wilderness is always an indication of incompetence, and I have no reason to disagree.

Chapter 28

Bull's-Eyes and Clay Pigeons

In the hands of ignorant or careless individuals a rifle is a dangerous weapon, likely to injure or kill the users and anyone else within range. Not only is the bullet apt to do harm, but the gun itself, improperly used, can blow up and cause great damage.

But when a rifle is utilized correctly, and the proper precautions are taken, shooting it is far safer than playing football, even baseball, and certainly safer than driving a car.

Almost all firearm accidents happen because the user didn't know it was loaded, through horseplay, or because the gun is permitted to be handled by someone uninformed or heedless. Col. Townsend Whelen impressed this upon me when I first began to shoot and hunt, and says it better in his now out-of-print book, *The Hunting Rifle,* than I know of anywhere else.

"Throughout all my life a large and increasing number of red-blooded Americans have been striving to make us a 'Nation of Riflemen,'" he says. "We have succeeded. May we ever remain thus, for the privilege to bear and the ability to use weapons is the greatest guarantee of liberty.. . .

"It is also, as it was to our forefathers who made this continent's frontiers liveable, in some ways the most instinctive, stirring, and challenging satisfaction any of us can ever know in the outdoors.''

Like most other things in life, safe firearm handling starts with common sense and continues with the resulting logical habits that develop. These begin with assuming every gun is loaded, and when others don't, getting out of their way.

It is only reasonable never to handle any gun, even an antique, without first checking for ammunition in the magazine. Also, particularly check the barrel, to make sure that it is unobstructed if the piece will be fired and that the chamber is empty. If there's any doubt about the chamber, feel this opening with the little finger.

When you don't have enough know-how with a particular weapon, and there are hundreds of varieties, have someone qualified do the verifying before you, after watching, take over.

As for keeping the muzzle always pointed in the safest direction, this is not always downward.

DOWN OR UP

Although it's often safer as well as faster in hunting country to bring your gun down on the target, some ranges are so built that insofar as precaution is involved the opposite is true.

Lifting the weapon up to the line of sight on such ranges means that a shot jerked off accidentally is more likely to go harmlessly into the ground in front of the target, rather than above it where people and property may be endangered.

HALF-SAFE IS UNSAFE

Whether within the crowded practice and competitive limits or alone in the wilds, everybody's continued well-being can depend on never relying on any mechanical device to be foolproof. Firearm safeties not only occasionally slip, but more often the more accessible ones are thumbed off unconsciously, two reasons for using any safety only as one part of prudent gun handling.

A third reason is that safeties and triggers on bolt action rifles can in some instances be manipulated in such a way that the gun fires when the safety is released. An accidental discharge also can sometimes be caused by moving the safety between the fire and safe positions, pressing the trigger, and then shifting the safety to the firing position.

The admonition to keep the safety on until the moment of firing is not always sound, either. When wounded or, on occasion, cornered big game is close, especially in thick cover, the stay-alive maneuver can be keeping the safety off and the ready forefinger positioned against the outside front of the trigger guard until the decisive moment.

As for hunting with the chamber empty, in some country this often means that when game suddenly comes into sight, you may unnecessarily alert it when you move a cartridge into place, waste more time getting set while the quarry already is starting away, and then maybe end up squeezing the trigger with the safety still on.

With revolvers in which direct pressure against the hammer can detonate a cartridge beneath, most experienced handlers choose to keep this compartment empty. With an otherwise full cylinder, the possible shots are only reduced by one.

In open country where big game shooting can be deliberate, hunters carrying in their saddle scabbard a lever action rifle or carbine that has an exposed hammer usually empty the chamber before sheathing the gun—a good idea with these models in such circumstances anywhere.

SAFE HANDLING IN ANY AREA

Everywhere it's important to keep weapons pointed in the safest direction, which isn't always down and sometimes isn't up. Such caution logically continues when guns are put aside, at which times again depending on the circumstances, safety is not necessarily greater when they are empty.

Leaned shotguns and rifles too often dangerously slide or become dislodged. Sights, if nothing more serious happens, are also knocked hazardously awry when hurrying shooters prop their firearms against the particularly slippery automobiles.

Later, getting these arms over and through fences with more hurry then worry, racks up its victims. As for horseplay, alcohol, and ingredients in even some over-the-counter medicines—these and firearms never have been compatible.

THE DANGERS IN DIFFERENT LOADS

Gunpowder can cause almost incomprehensible destruction. If it is improperly confined by hand-loading too heavy a charge, by having thick grease or some other obstruction in the bore, or as it is when the wrong cartridge is fired, it may detonate with fiendish power.

The most common reason such accidents occur is that some ammunition can be readily inserted and fired in guns for which it was never intended. Correct cartridge interchangeability is limited, and doing it may be extremely unsafe.

For example, a .357 Magnum chamber will accept both the .30 Special and the .38 Long Colt cartridges. But a .357 Magnum cartridge should never be used in a gun chambered only for a .38 Special or .38 Long Colt. Although ordinarily it won't slip into the chamber, some of the older .38 Long Colt weapons will accept this .357 Magnum charge. Firing any with such a load may be one's last time around.

Also, the cartridge for the 7.9-millimeter German Mauser military can be inserted and fired in the .30-caliber Army rifle. To the uninitiated the two cartridges look alike. Yet the German cartridge will completely demolish the United States rifle, and duplicate conditions in other firearms will do the same.

ONE, TWO, THREE, FOUR

When a shooter, as happens occasionally, loads and attempts to fire the wrong shell or cartridge in a firearm, one of four things usually happens: The action can't be closed, and the mistake is at once discovered. The load slips beyond the reach of the firing pin, but not deeply enough to permit a second to be chambered behind it. An undersized load lodges in the barrel, setting up a very dangerous obstruction because then a second load can be chambered and fired. An example is the familiar 20-12-gauge shotgun barrel burst. Or, an incorrect cartridge of the wrong caliber, wrong case dimensions, or both becomes seated in the chamber and is detonated, whereupon if only the gun is damaged, everyone about is lucky.

Although ammunition mismatching can occur with all types of firearms, the potential is greatest with center fire loads, mainly from failure to become aware of, and to use, the correct and complete cartridge designation when ordering or selecting cartridges. Numerous center fire cartridges have been designed and are still being produced, including variations of the same caliber (or diameter), but with otherwise different dimensions.

THE RISKY LACK OF A COMMON STANDARD

Although no common standard yet exists for naming cartridges, numbers are always used to indicate the caliber, often in conjunction with words or other numbers so as to differentiate them. The numbers may be decimal fractions of an inch, such as .30 caliber, although more and more they are given in millimeters in deference to the metric system.

There's certain confusion here, too, as when the .219 zipper appeared. It is .22 caliber or rather .224 caliber—almost all so-called .22-caliber cartridges are really .224 caliber.

These cartridges are .30 caliber: 30 Remington, 30/30 Winchester, 30/06 Springfield, 30/40 Krag, 300 Savage, 300 Winchester Magnum, and 300 H&H Magnum. These are .28 caliber: 280 Remington, 284 Winchester, 7-millimeter Express Remington, 7-millimeter Mauser, 7-millimeter–08 Remington, 7-millimeter Weatherby Magnum, and 7-millimeter Remington Magnum.

It's obviously critical for the shooter to know, at the least, the exact and full cartridge designation for which his rifle is chambered, to use this when buying ammunition, and then to double-check the flap of each box after purchasing and again before using.

The 7-millimeter Mauser cartridge will fit into rifles chambered for the 8-millimeter Mauser, 270 Winchester, 7-millimeter Express Remington, 280 Remington, and 284 Winchester. A rifle chambered for the 7-millimeter Remington Magnum will accept such incorrect cartridges as the 270 Winchester, 7-millimeter Weatherby Magnum, 280 Remington, 7-millimeter Express Remington, 7-millimeter–08 Remington, 35 Remington, and 350 Remington Magnum.

UNDULY HAZARDOUS

Unless the shooter knows what he or she is doing, firing any ammunition in a weapon not specifically designed and chambered for it is almost always unduly hazardous. So is using an old firearm when you are uncertain about its condition or the identity of the ammunition for which it was designed and constructed.

Shotguns with Damascus or twist steel barrels can be unsafe with any of today's shells containing either black or smokeless powder.

Other stay-safe precautions are to keep ammunition either in its original box or in a container marked with its correct and complete name. Then in the field there's never a danger of mixing shells of different gauges in the same pocket.

GOOD SHOTS ARE NOT BORN BUT MADE

In the first place, there is no such thing as a born shot. As Colonel Whelen puts it, the average American tends to think he inherits skills with guns from his ancestors, and that all he needs to make himself a fine shot is a little practice "to get his eye in, all absolute bunk!"

Unguided practice simply develops bad habits that will probably preclude you from ever becoming a good shot, or at least make it more difficult for you to become one.

"Several years ago, returning from the northern wilderness," Colonel Whelen recounted, "I met a sportsman who had just been on an unsuccessful moose hunt. He wanted to know where he could get tracer bullets to see where his shots were going.

"A few nights ago I read a typical book on African shooting. The first thing the mighty nimrods did after reaching 'the dark continent' was 'sight in their rifles.' Then they proceeded to miss or merely wound 70 percent of the game they shot at within easy ranges. I tabulated all the shooting recorded to get this average.

"This, like many similar hunting books, is full of such remarks as: 'Something gone wrong with the sights,' 'My eye was off,' 'I missed five oribi point blank,' 'I fired seven shots at an ostrich sixty yards away,' 'The best shots do extraordinary things here,' and 'We all have our off days.'

"Now to a trained rifleman every one of these quoted remarks marks the writer as an absolute tyro with a rifle—he has not even begun to learn. For be it known that a trained rifleman knows where his bullets are going, something does not go wrong with the sights, his eye is never off except by booze or illness, he does not miss five of anything point blank.

"An ostrich presents almost a two-foot target, and he could not well miss it at sixty yards unless he was panting hard from exertion, or had 'buck fever' which he does not have because he has confidence in himself. He does have his off days, but they consist of times when his shooting perhaps enlarges his ordinary group by about an inch at a hundred yards. Big game is ridiculously easy for him to hit at any sporting distance."

INTELLIGENT PRACTICE PLUS EXPERIENCE

"The actual facts are that the average sportsman who takes his 'trusty' rifle in hand but once a year, and many who have hunted for a decade, are complete duffers with the rifle," Colonel Whelen noted.

"Despite what many of them term their 'wide experience' and their self-styled 'ability as game shots,' they have no knowledge or skill with the rifle and its use. In most cases they have a terrible lot of misinformation, plus a lot of fixed bad habits. When a beginner talks to such a sportsman he often absorbs a lot of bunk.

"The instant these individuals take a rifle in their hands they make precisely the same example of themselves that the fellow does who has a golf club in his hands for the first time. The golfer probably makes a swing at the ball and digs up a square foot of sod. The beginner in shooting, or the person who has shot long and poorly, handles his rifle in such a way that it is not necessary for a rifleman to see him shoot to estimate his performance correctly.

"Shooting is just as much a science as golf, tennis, football, or billiards. A beginner will be just as hopeless at the start as he will when he first takes up any other game of skill. Like other sports, it can be learned only by a study of the technique and then practice, and expertness depends upon intelligent practice plus experience.

"It is not absolutely impossible to learn to shoot well without a good book or coach. Some few have done it by grovelling in the dark, stumbled on the truth, or evolved it by elimination, brainwork, and tenacity. But such individuals are scarce, and what a lot of time they lost by disregarding the experience of others, and how prodigious their labors were."

SO THE EARS CAN HEAR

Without ear protection, continued exposure to the immediate sound of shooting increasingly diminishes hearing acuity. This progresses with the most debilitation among sportsmen and sportswomen during trap, skeet, and target firing.

Another disability often arises at the same time: Shooters develop accuracy-wrecking flinch from muzzle blast far more frequently than from recoil.

The most certain safeguard against the effects of such percussion is acoustical earmuffs, particularly those which also cover the bone area behind the ears.

Even wads of cotton work handily for the casual shooter who's busting clay pigeons or adjusting a telescopic sight. They reduce the impact on the inner ear of sound concussion without eliminating the ability to hear normal conversation.

Sonic ear valves, with ball bearings which block sudden blasts while not interfering with everyday noises, are the choice of some of the big game outfitters in remote mountain regions. There, otherwise, progressing deafness is a common result of being within inches of too many high magnum rifles, fired at sheep and goat to which the outfitter or guide is pointing.

IGNORANCE HASN'T PREVENTED MISHAPS YET

A common cause of accidents is leaving a firearm where a young person, who usually turns out to be a boy, can get hold of it, and almost all such accidents are chargeable to the adults involved.

Reasonably, young individuals ordinarily should not be denied firearms at a proper age, because a gun has an irresistible attraction for particularly every boy, Colonel Whelen believes. Sooner or later he is going to get hold of one, with or without permission.

"Far better with permission," as Colonel Whelen points out, "and after proper instruction!"

Children, once they can reason, are never too young to start recognizing gun safety. When they see adults consistently treating firearms with respect, they're likely to follow such practice naturally. As their inborn curiosity increases, it's realistic to take them one day where it is safe and fire one or two rounds of high velocity ammunition into closed gallon cans of water, or something like this where the consequences will be similarly impressive, to let them hear and see what really happens.

Keeping young people unenlightened not only ensures they will not understand the potential dangers, but also increases the likelihood they'll seek to satisfy their inquisitiveness when there isn't suitable supervision.

The hazards which the adult wants to eliminate are enormously increased if the young person does not know the way firearms function. In many areas at least part of the answer can be the satisfaction and the responsibility generated in one of the numerous firearm safety classes sponsored by sportsmen and sportswomen throughout the United States and Canada.

THE NONPOWDER GUNS

Perhaps one of the things you also learned in your early teens with a Daisy BB gun and later a higher velocity Crosman air gun—while enjoying the satisfaction, with thousands of inexpensive shots, of learning how to hit more challenging targets later—is that sport shooting should be avoided unless you are sure the projectile will come to a safe stop.

Coming to realize this way also that ricochets are always dangerous, you, too, may have started discovering the smoothness there can be in swinging with moving objects, such as tossed tin cans, that makes graduation to the ultimate targets of trap, skeet, and wing shooting an almost effortless transition.

Air rifle and air pistol competition is being added to the 1984 Olympics. Their impact on American lifestyles, though, may perhaps be better appreciated when it's realized that Daisy, the world's oldest and largest manufacturer of nonpowder guns and ammunition, has produced twenty million pump-action BB guns since 1914.

Among the precision air-powered weapons, many of the pneumatic rifles and particularly the pistols have internal mechanisms considerably more complicated than those in the firearms on which they are modeled. It follows that they merit no less respect, not only in care and maintenance, but in all other matters involving safety. This is especially evident in the high velocity Crosmen rifles and pistols, monitored by the Coleman Company, that are powered with compressed carbon dioxide.

THE BEST ALL-AROUND WEAPON

If you want an all-around weapon you can depend on for both large and small game in the United States and Canada, your most practical choice is one of the better bolt-action rifles using a cartridge of .270, .30, 7-millimeter, or comparable caliber with both the necessary power and flat trajectory.

The fired cartridge cases then can be reloaded with suitable powder charges and bullets, which can be relied upon to shoot where you aim at short range for smaller game, with the sights remaining adjusted to strike at point of aim at two hundred yards, the greatest sure-hitting range for sheep, moose, and grizzly.

The small loads should be adequate for all of your area's legal meat, from partridge to the crows sometimes marketed as rooks, and from pheasant to the really delectable muskrats you may have seen sold as marsh rabbits.

The most satisfactory light loads use jacketed bullets with sharp points. Such a bullet will not expand at low velocity. Passing through the body of a grouse or a lynx, it will neither waste too much meat nor destroy a trophy pelt.

Colonel Whelen used such a load in his .30-06 hunting rifle with the most complete satisfaction during the last half-century of his outdoor life. Specifically, it consists of a hand-loaded 150-grain, full-jacketed, pointed M11 service bullet with a powder charge of 18 grains of DuPont No. 4759 powder. Even better loads, he told me, are the .25-caliber,

87-grain and the .270-caliber, 110-grain bullets with slightly lighter charges of the same powder.

The best survival weapon you can carry, following the Stefansson-proved ounce of ammunition per ounce of meat criterion, is a light, hard-hitting, scope-sighted, bolt action rifle such as the Winchester Model 70.

This, when a heavy enough bullet is placed accurately in the chest cavity, will kill any American or Canadian big game and with a shoulder-crippling shot will also anchor it. A well-constructed .30-caliber bullet of 180 grains at a muzzle velocity of 2,700 feet a second will be adequate.

A handgun is lighter and more conveniently carried, except that is cannot be depended on to get the job done, when the one caribou whose meat you need to keep from starving may be the only animal you'll see for a week.

Throughout this continent north of the tropics I have found a .30-06 sufficient. If you are with a party, each member may well carry the same model rifle in this class, so that one will always be operative, and because there is nothing better.

Chapter 29

The Narrow Arrow

Archery with its more than five and a half million participants at last count now ranks twenty-seventh in popularity among the Americans of both sexes presently taking part in outdoor sports. A longer open season in certain areas is a contributing factor. In Michigan alone, licensed bowhunters have grown from 110 thousand to 205 thousand in two years.

The sport is safer than ever with the newer weaponry. It has always in some ways been more of a challenge than shooting a gun. Its more interested enthusiasts discover that getting their deer with bow and arrow brings with it a pioneer-like sense of accomplishment.

Today the most frequent cause of death among bowhunters is falling on arrows, says Glenn Helgeland who moved up from the National Wildlife Federation to become for a time the editor of *Archery World*. The remedy he suggests is never to carry them in your hand, and not even to walk with an arrow on your bowstring until the decisive moment of coming up on game.

He recommends keeping the arrows instead in a quiver which covers the broadheads completely, protection which not all quivers on today's market are deep enough to provide. Yet so guarding these

167

shafted missiles, which like other weapons are things to treat with regard for their hazard potential, also means the bowhunter's fingers will not be as likely cut by accidently grabbing one of the sharp heads when reaching for an arrow.

While waiting in a tree stand at a likely crossing or lick, keeping the deciding arrow in one of the several holding devices stocked by outfitters can prevent it from falling and perhaps sticking upright in the ground immediately below. Some bowhunters have themselves slipped next and landed on such arrows.

Archery is so relaxing, Mr. Helgeland says, that especially on drowsy fall days the bowhunter may do well to secure himself or herself, if only by an improvised safety belt, in any high vantage.

ARCHERY ELBOW

Although epicondylitis of the region is popularly known as tennis elbow, it is also produced by archery. This strain shows up in muscular tenderness, swelling, and sometimes a dangerously weakening grip.

What works best is rubbing the elbow vigorously at the trouble spot for several minutes whenever the discomfort begins. Dr. James A. Nicholas finds most patients who conscientiously relax the muscle tendon unit this way can be assured the trouble will clear completely within three to four months, or at least become less bothersome.

Even when it is believed injections may help, his experience is that one or two are sufficient, rather than the series currently in vogue.

Bandaging can help prevent pain with archery elbow. Dr. Nicholas suggests a simple exercise which often benefits the entire condition: With a strong rubber band around your fingertips, try spreading and then relaxing the fingers one hundred times or as often as is comfortable. As the disability improves, stronger elastics can be added advantageously to provide more resistance.

Chapter 30

The Roughest Fun You'll Ever Smooth

The actual challenge in the unpeopled places is "smoothing" rather than "roughing it," although with many of us "roughing it" was a memorable experience. But a lot of us, too, already have it rough enough in the crowded places!

The primary determinant of outdoor comfort, as it has been since the beginning of time, is the weather.

SPOTTING YOUR OWN WEATHER WARNINGS

It's been going on so long that, not surprisingly, sudden atmospheric changes that can kill you back of beyond are conditons you usually can spot well in advance. It is a matter of heeding the natural alerts which outdoors are about you everywhere. This becomes more urgent when several such indicators appear together.

Keeping on the watch on your own, and then doing something about it, will likely mean you'll never be the someone strayed or stranded in a blizzard—and making things worse by an ill-timed attempt to walk out instead of safely waiting it out in an improvised, fire-cheered shelter.

Even campfire smoke carries its portent, spreading downward

after that initial lift with hot air, when heavy weather is lingering and, more ominously, when it is approaching. Rising straight up, smoke's message is fair conditions.

A red sun or sky at dawn foretells nearing disturbance. The same color at sunset, though, affirms the air is carrying so little moisture that rain or snow within the next twenty-four hours is highly improbable.

Dew and frost appear in sparkling abundance, too, only when the air is so dry that precipitation is unlikely. When they fail to heavy the ground cover during a still night, generally rain or snow is close.

As stormy weather nears, canvas and axheads tighten in the thickening humidity. Well in advance, spiders stop spinning their low webs.

THE HUNTER'S AIR DRIFT

Mist rising mornings from canyons and hollows in high country augurs fine weather. So, as the hunter particularly notices, do air currents that sift downward as the sun rises and drift back up at dusk. When these thermal currents reverse, it's an omen of coming storm.

The higher the clouds, the better the weather, especially when they're scattered in brilliant clear blueness and becoming fewer. Drifting together in an already milky sky, they presage conditions not so promising. So do tight thin clouds gathering gradually about the moon during a course of fair days and nights.

The same is true any time only a few stars glimmer. It is the uncloaked night alive with the some two thousand visible stars that is the favored soothsayer, unless what you want is tracking snow.

STARS, SAND, AND FLOOD

In the windy places on the high North American deserts, where the blowing sands sing, the stars are eloquent.

Here as soon as the sun disappears below the dunes, night characteristically becomes chilly enough for a lightweight down jacket or at least a wool shirt. Later, the shadowy bottom of a yard-deep slit can be 100°F. cooler than the temperature on the sun-scorched surface. When there's no other shade, scooping such a niche in an east-west line may save your life one day.

If a sandstorm sweeps upon you while you're perhaps walking out toward the mountains, and to be safe multiplying your estimations of distance by three, try to get in the lee of a rise. There, mark your direction with anything handy, and sit with your back to the turbulence and a handkerchief over your nose and mouth. Storing the leisure, with its minimal functional and metabolic activity that the desert windstorm is making available, may later make the difference.

There need be none of the uninformed worry about being buried. Besides reducing body water loss, the sand in which some desert survivors have buried themsleves deliberately has proved relaxing, refreshing, and on occasion reinvigorating to a surprising degree.

The tempting undercut bank of a dry stream bed is never as safe, then or for camping later, as even a remote cloud burst can bring the sudden overwhelming surge of a flood.

V

GETTING IT ALL TOGETHER

The knowledge you absorb today will have added to it the knowledge you will absorb tomorrow, and on your capacity for absorption, and not on any fixed standard, will depend the amount of knowledge you will ultimately accumulate. And at the end of the accumulating period—be that period one year or fifty—you will find that you are only at the beginning, and that the whole field of nature lies before you waiting to be explored.

Jim Corbett

Chapter 31

The Added Security in Becoming a Winner

Opinions differ at least as often as the viewpoints on which they are based, yet few will disagree that physical deficiencies and handicaps can be overcome and sometimes even turned into assets.

It is also widely accepted that each outdoor activity has its particular demands, which every participant answers in line with his or her ability. The five most frequently involved essentials have proved to be timing, coordination, accuracy, discipline, and practice.

Timing, one of the more important and an often required performance factor, seems best developed through practice. Even the alertness which holds everything together is a result of training, which usually can still sharpen alertness more.

Rhythm, a trait common to all sports, is also something most can develop. Even agility is defined as a quality that improves with practice.

Steadiness, the ability to control the mental and physical facilities while seeking maximum efficiency during all situations encountered within the body and the surrounding environment, is largely built on experience.

A major physical advantage women have over men is flexibility.

Most can acquire strength. The combination of both is what, regardless of sex or sport, makes the superior athlete.

When both genders enter the thirty-five to fifty-five age group, the prime earning years, they can compete just as intensely as their younger fellows, but at greater risk because of decreasing agility, coordination, steadiness, accuracy, and endurance. This is often offset by participating in less demanding recreation. A major problem over fifty-five is that partly because of fading muscle tone, achievement becomes increasingly difficult, setting up dangers when it is pursued with the same determination. But the natural competitive instinct does not diminish. Fortunately, it can be tempered by an enriching philosophical outlook.

At the dusk of time, one fact no doubt present at its dawn will probably still be with us—that some of our most memorable moments occur during diversions which seem at their start the least consequential.

All along, efficiency increases with achievement. Safest still are the skills it takes to succeed. And success in one phase of living is accompanied almost always by success in nearly everything else.

Index